First World War
and Army of Occupation
War Diary
France, Belgium and Germany

36 DIVISION
107 Infantry Brigade,
Brigade Machine Gun Company
18 December 1915 - 31 January 1918

WO95/2503/6

The Naval & Military Press Ltd
www.nmarchive.com
Published in association with The National Archives

Published by

The Naval & Military Press Ltd

Unit 10 Ridgewood Industrial Park,

Uckfield, East Sussex,

TN22 5QE England

Tel: +44 (0) 1825 749494

www.naval-military-press.com

www.nmarchive.com

This diary has been reprinted in facsimile from the original. Any imperfections are inevitably reproduced and the quality may fall short of modern type and cartographic standards.

© **Crown Copyright**
Images reproduced by permission of The National Archives, London, England, 2015.

Contents

Document type	Place/Title	Date From	Date To
Heading	WO95/2503/6 Brigade Machine Gun Company		
Heading	36th Division 107th Infy Bde 107th Machine Gun Coy. 1915 Dec-Jan 1918		
Heading	36 Div 107 Bde 4th Division War Diaries 107th Bde. M.G.C. December To January 1915-16		
Heading	107th Inf Bde. 4th Division. 107th Brigade Machine Gun Company December 1915		
Heading	War Diary Of 107th Brigade Machine Gun Company From 18th Dec 1915 To 31st Dec 1915		
War Diary	Forceville	18/12/1915	30/12/1915
War Diary	Mailly Maillet	31/12/1915	31/12/1915
Heading	107th Inf Bde 4th Division. 107th Brigade Machine Gun Company January 1916		
Heading	War Diary Of 107th Brigade Machine Gun Company From 1st To 31st January 1916		
War Diary	Mailly Maillet	01/01/1916	31/01/1916
Heading	War Diary Of 107th Brigade Machine Gun Company From 1st To 29th February 1916		
War Diary	Mailly Maillet	01/02/1916	29/02/1916
Heading	War Diary Of 107th Coy Machine Gun Corps From 1st To 31st March 1916 Vol 4		
War Diary	Mailly Maillet	01/03/1916	30/03/1916
Heading	War Diary Of 107 Coy Machine Gun Corps From 1st April To 29th April 1916 Vol 5		
War Diary	Mailly Maillet	01/04/1916	06/04/1916
War Diary	Puchvillers	07/04/1916	20/04/1916
War Diary	Varennes	21/04/1916	29/04/1916
War Diary	Varennes	01/05/1916	08/05/1916
War Diary	Martinsart Wood	09/05/1916	31/05/1916
Heading	107th Brigade. 36th Division. 107th Machine Gun Company June 1916		
War Diary	Martinsart Wood	01/06/1916	31/06/1916
Heading	107th Brigade. 36th Division. 107th Brigade Machine Gun Company July 1916		
Miscellaneous	D.A.G., G.H.Q., 3rd Echelon.	29/08/1916	29/08/1916
War Diary		01/07/1916	31/07/1916
War Diary	Bulford Camp	01/08/1916	30/09/1916
Miscellaneous	107th Inf Bde	01/11/1916	01/11/1916
War Diary		01/10/1916	31/10/1916
War Diary	Bulford Camp	01/11/1916	31/01/1917
War Diary	In The Field	01/02/1917	06/04/1917
War Diary	Trenches Spanbroek Molen Sector	07/04/1917	10/04/1917
War Diary	In The Trenches Spanbroek Molen Sector	11/04/1917	15/04/1917
War Diary	In The Trenches Spanbroek Sector	16/04/1917	20/04/1917
War Diary	Training Area Leval D'Acquin	21/04/1917	30/04/1917
War Diary	In The Field	01/05/1917	16/05/1917
War Diary	In The Trenches	17/05/1917	17/05/1917
War Diary	Spanbroek Sector	17/05/1917	20/05/1917
War Diary	In The Field	21/05/1917	26/05/1917
War Diary	Spanbroek Sector	27/05/1917	29/05/1917

War Diary	In The Trenches	30/05/1917	30/05/1917
War Diary	Spanbroek Sector	31/05/1917	08/06/1917
War Diary	In The Field	09/06/1917	31/08/1917
Miscellaneous	107th Infantry Brigade. Report On Operations Of The Above Company On The 16th August, 1917	16/08/1917	16/08/1917
Miscellaneous	107th Infantry Brigade		
Miscellaneous	107th Infantry Brigade.		
Miscellaneous	107th Infantry Brigade	16/08/1917	16/08/1917
War Diary	In The Field	01/09/1917	18/09/1917
War Diary	Field	18/09/1917	31/10/1917
War Diary	In The Field	01/12/1917	21/12/1917
War Diary	Field	22/12/1917	31/01/1918

WO95/2503/6

Brigade Machine Gun Company

36TH DIVISION
107TH INFY BDE

107TH MACHINE GUN COY.
1915 DEC ~~FEB 1916~~ - JAN 1918

36 DIV
107 BDE

Attached 4th Division

War Diaries

107th Bde. M.G.C.

December, to January

1915 - 16

2304

107th **Inf** Bde.
4th Division.

107th BRIGADE MACHINE GUN COMPANY

DECEMBER 1915

CONFIDENTIAL

War Diary

of

107th Brigade Machine Gun Company

From 18th Dec. 1915 to 31st Dec 1915

(-1)

Army Form C. 2118.

WAR DIARY
or
INTELLIGENCE SUMMARY
(Erase heading not required.)

Place	Date	Hour	Summary of Events and Information	Remarks and references to Appendices
FORCEVILLE	18th Dec. 1915		The 107th Bde. M.G. Coy. formed from M.G. Sections of the following battalions.	
			8th R. Ir. Rifles	
			9th do	
			10th do	
			15th do	
			1/2nd MONMOUTHSHIRE REGT	
			Capt A.B. WOODGATE DSO. 1st EAST LANCS takes over command with the following Subalterns under him.	
			Lieut D Monaghan. 15th Royal Irish Rifles	
			" C.A. Jackson. 8th do	
			" E Coey 15th do	
			" A.L. Stewart. 10th do	
			" J.H. Fraser 1/2nd Monmouthshire Regt	Ees.
			" C.R. Sanderson. 9th Royal Irish Rifles	
			" Hoope 9th do	
			2/Lt " J Mourn 10th do	
			" S Gault 10th do	
			Lieut Graden proceeds on leave.	

2449 Wt. W14957/M90 750,000 1/16 J.B.C. & A. Forms/C.2118/12.

Army Form C. 2118.

WAR DIARY.
or
INTELLIGENCE SUMMARY

(Erase heading not required.)

Instructions regarding War Diaries and Intelligence Summaries are contained in F. S. Regs., Part II. and the Staff Manual respectively. Title Pages will be prepared in manuscript.

Place	Date	Hour	Summary of Events and Information	Remarks and references to Appendices
FORCEVILLE	Dec 22nd 1915		Eight Officers Chargers arrive.	W.
	23rd		All 16 Guns go into trenches taking over from the 10th Brigade M.G. Coy.	W.
	24th		Conference of O.C.s of B.M.G. Coys of 4th Div. at ACHEUX. 10th Company Officially formed. Vide 4th Div. R.O. 1080. 27/12/15	W.
	25th		Relief takes place — Hand over to 10th B.M.G. Coy. Shrub & Smith reports from Base.	W.
	29th		Relief Vide over from 10th Pagan M.G. Coy	W.
	30th		Lieut Steward proceeds on leave.	W.
MAILLY MAILLET	31st		Headquarters removed from FORCEVILLE to Billet 76 in MAILLY MAILLET.	W.

107th Inf Bde

4th Division.

107th BRIGADE MACHINE GUN COMPANY

JANUARY 1916

CONFIDENTIAL

War Diary.

107th Brigade Machine Gun Company.

From 1st to 31st January 1916

Army Form C. 2118.

WAR DIARY
or
INTELLIGENCE SUMMARY

(Erase heading not required.)

Place	Date	Hour	Summary of Events and Information	Remarks and references to Appendices
MAILLY MAILLET	1916 Jan 1.		Brigades to carry out their own reliefs. The 19th Brigade to take over North of the SERRE Road. The 107th Brigade to take South of the SERRE ROAD. The Bde M.G. Coy to have 8 guns in and 8 guns out. The guns north of the SERRE Road are withdrawn and emplacement handed over to the 19th Brigade. 19th Brigade emplacement handed over. 2 emplacements in AUCHONVILLERS from the MONMOUTHSHIRE Regt. Lieut COEY sick to hospital	C21
				C21
	3rd		Relief carried out. Lieut JACKSON goes on leave	
	5th		Guns in PRETTY ST and KING ST brought back to the Divn Line of PILLIS SQUARE & FORT HOYSTED and replaced by 1/2 MONMOUTH Lewis guns. Only Vickers guns to be in Divisional line	C23
	6th		1st EAST LANCS on our right in front of HAMEL heavily shelled	
	7th		Relief carried out	
	10th		Lieut ALSTEWART returning from leave & Lt MONAGHAN goes on leave. Lt GESANDERSON takes over Job of actg adjutant Sir DOUGLAS HAIG visits MAILLY	C24
	11th		Relief carried out. Dugout in the TENDERLOIN called THE NICKERAGE taken over by No Company	C24

Army Form C. 2118.

WAR DIARY
or
INTELLIGENCE SUMMARY

(Erase heading not required.)

Instructions regarding War Diaries and Intelligence Summaries are contained in F. S. Regs., Part II. and the Staff Manual respectively. Title Pages will be prepared in manuscript.

Place	Date	Hour	Summary of Events and Information	Remarks and references to Appendices
MAILLY MAILLET	1916 Jan 12th		Lt D MOORE attached to Company from 15th R.I. Rifles to replace Lt COEY who goes to AUCHONVILLERS. Takes over Command of the two Guns there	CEL
	15th	3 30pm	Practice on the range with No 1 & 2. Gas return. 20 men of 8th R.I. Rifles to dig communication 2/Lt MARTIN takes VALLADE CORNER to FREDDY STREET trench from	
			Lt FRASER with an N.C.O & 10 men after dark cleared the covered way to FORT FRASER and cleaned up emplacement. FORT FRASER is the emplacement by the signpost at the junction of the SUNKEN RD & NEW BEAUMONT RD	CEL
	15th		Lt JACKSON returns from leave arrived at ACHEUX the previous night	CEL
	16th		Relief cancelled out	CEL
	17th		2/Lt MARTIN & 2/Lt GAULT go on leave	CEL
			Engineers complete dugout at FORT HOYSTED working parties saw to dugout in the TENDERLOIN and to FORT FRASER	CEL
	18th			CEL
	20th		Lt COEY returned from hospital Lt MONAGHAN returns from leave.	CEL

WAR DIARY
or
INTELLIGENCE SUMMARY
(Erase heading not required.)

Army Form C. 2118.

Place	Date	Hour	Summary of Events and Information	Remarks and references to Appendices
MAILLY MAILLET	1916 Jan. 21.		Relief takes place. LT STEWART MOORE to TENDERLOIN and LT MONAGHAN to AUCHONVILLERS.	C.O.S
	22nd		Brackets for officers chargers brought up from FORCEVILLE.	C.O.S
	24th		Stake to be erected in MAILLY wood.	
			No 16025 Pte TURKINGTON W & No 13876 Pte WILSON H Severely injured owing to an explosion caused by a rifle grenade detonator. Capt. WOODGATE proceeds on leave. LT MONAGHAN takes over Command of the Company. Court of Enquiry on Pte TURKINGTON WILSON.	C.O.S
	25th		Presidency LT WH FRASER Members. LT CA JACKSON. and LT GE SANDERSON. Court finds that injuries are due to the negligence of Pte WILSON.	C.O.S
	26th		Relief takes place.	
	27th		Test with handcarts carried out. No 5 Gun under LT FRASER goes to FORT FRASER & gets into action in 32 minutes No 6 Gun under LT GE SANDERSON. goes to No4 Emplacement in 5 AVENUE gets into action in 36 minutes	C.O.S
		7.30. PM	Gas Alarm. Church bell rung. all stand to 2 Guns were ready to move off on the handcarts in less than 5 minutes. After about half an hour alarm reported false.	C.O.S

Army Form C. 2118.

WAR DIARY
or
INTELLIGENCE SUMMARY

(Erase heading not required.)

Instructions regarding War Diaries and Intelligence Summaries are contained in F. S. Regs., Part II. and the Staff Manual respectively. Title Pages will be prepared in manuscript.

Place	Date	Hour	Summary of Events and Information	Remarks and references to Appendices
MAILLY MAILLET	1916 Jan. 28th	8 AM	A second gas alarm. All stood to. Two guns on road cart ready to move off. All men medically inspected	Bd
	29th	7AM	A third gas alarm. Nothing further occurred. The RE constructing new emplacement at the CRUCIFIX. No. 16694 Pte McAllen A has self inflicted injury to right thumb. Court of Enquiry held. Was injury due to negligence. Lt Martin returned from leave.	Bd
	30th	4 PM	A fourth gas alarm	Bd
	31st		Reliefs take place	Bd

CONFIDENTIAL

War Diary.
of
107th Brigade Machine Gun Company

From 1st to 20th February 1916

WAR DIARY
or
INTELLIGENCE SUMMARY

(Erase heading not required.)

Army Form C. 2118.

Place	Date	Hour	Summary of Events and Information	Remarks and references to Appendices
MAILLY MAILLET	1916 Feb. 1st		LT SANDERSON proceeds on leave. LT FRASER takes over duties of Adjutant. Transport brought up from FORCEVILLE to MAILLY Wood	S21.
	3rd		Leave stopped.	E21
	4th		Relief took place. 36th Divn takes over the line from KING ST. VALLADE Company takes over two new gun positions KING ST. VALLADE in addition to those already held	E21
	5th		Enemy Aeroplane drops bombs in MAILLY which kills one man & two horses.	E21
	7th		LT JACKSON proceeds to LEALVILLERS. Sick to hospital	E21
	11th		LT SANDERSON returns from leave takes over duties of adjutant	E21
	12½		Capt WOODGATE Severely wounded by a shell whilst walking through AUCHONVILLERS The PARKER wounded whilst gathering buds in AUCHONVILLERS	E21
	14th		Court Martial on 9th 16694 Pte McALLEN H. He is found guilty and sentenced to 6 months imprisonment with hard labour. This sentence is commuted by the Brigadier to three months F.P. No 1.	E21
	15th		Relief night. The 109th M G Coy send 5 N.C. os. & 10 O.R. for instruction with our men. This enables us to relieve	E21
	16th		all 10 Gun teams Pump our cellar under Pallor 79.	

Army Form C. 2118.

WAR DIARY
or
INTELLIGENCE SUMMARY

(Erase heading not required.)

Place	Date	Hour	Summary of Events and Information	Remarks and references to Appendices
MAILLY MAILLET	10/16 Feb 18th			
	19th		Reinforcements report from GRANTHAM. Enemy makes an attack on the 12 Bgde on our right. We get alarm & send down guns down to the battle emplacement. After about an hour these guns are withdrawn and nothing further occurs.	Z2.1
	20th		Sergeants Mess started	Z2.1
	22nd		3 Officer returns from leave	Z2.1
	24th		Take over Buller 87. All leave stopped	Z2.1
	25th		Capt A.G. KEYSER takes over command of the Company. Heavy fall of snow. Autogun arrives. Motor line frozen. Owing to 100th Bgde M.G. Coy owing to just unable to get mules on the road & reliefs are cancelled our on the road carts	Z2.1
	27th		Thaw commences. All Lorries off roads, rations brought up to LEALVILLERS by horse transport.	Z2.1
	28th		Brig Gen: WITHYCOMB near MAILLY sheds sections at drill	Z2.1

2449 Wt. W14957/M90 750,000 1/16 J.B.C. & A. Forms/C.2118/12.

107 MG Coy
Vol 4

~~XXXVI~~

CONFIDENTIAL

War Diary
of
107th Coy. Machine Gun Corps

From 1st to 31st March 1916

WAR DIARY
or
INTELLIGENCE SUMMARY

(Erase heading not required.)

Army Form C. 2118.

Place	Date	Hour	Summary of Events and Information	Remarks and references to Appendices
MAILLY- MAILLET	1916 MAR. 1st		Four reinforcements arrive from Grantham.	
	3rd		107th Brigade relieve the 109th Brigade	
	4th		107th Coy. M.G. Corps take over line from 109th Coy. M.G. Corps. 10 Men attached to Company as Carriers from Battalions of Brigade.	
	8th		1 Gun Team Captured by the Motor Machine Gun Battery. Heavy fall of Snow.	
	9th		Relief taken place. Two more men supplied by Battalions. Material for Officers dug out taken up to Tender Point. Work on South Chatham Empt.	
	10th		Take over Emergency Emplt. from XIV M.M.Gun Battery.	
	12th		Relief. Aeroplane dropped bomb on MAILLY.	
	13th	12.15am	One of our aeroplanes brought down by Machine Gun fire	
	14th		Work in South Chatham at night.	
	16th		Relief. Lt Sanderson goes into trenches. Lt Monaghan takes over duty as Adjutant	
	19th	2 a.m.	Our trenches heavily shelled. No casualties. Enemy raid trenches of Battalion on our left. 48th Division leave starts again. Tour of trenches extended to ten days.	
	20th		Work on S. Chatham. Corp. McAllister and L. Cpl. Watt proceeded on leave.	

Army Form C. 2118.

WAR DIARY
or
INTELLIGENCE SUMMARY
(Erase heading not required.)

Instructions regarding War Diaries and Intelligence Summaries are contained in F.S. Regs., Part II. and the Staff Manual respectively. Title Pages will be prepared in manuscript.

Place	Date	Hour	Summary of Events and Information	Remarks and references to Appendices
MAILLY - MAILLET	Mar 21st		Lieut Fraser relieves Lt Stewart in trenches.	
	22nd		Reliefs	
	24th		Leave stopped. Pte Turkington arrives from Base	
	26th		One reinforcement arrives from Grantham	
	27th		Official notice received that the Brigade will be relieved by the 93rd Inf Brigade	
	27th		Court Martial on No 13876 Pte Wilson for Neglijently wounding himself. Found guilty and sentenced to 3 Month F.P. No. 1.	
	28th		Lt. Sanderson goes into trenches and relieves Lt. Fraser. Lt. Coy comes out of trenches and relieves takes over duties of Transport Officer.	
	29th		Leave postponed one day. Move of Coy. postponed about the 5th April. Relief carried out. 9/Pte Kane wounded in leg by shell splinter. 93rd Brigade relieves 107th Bde.	
	30th		Advance party consisting of A section under Lieut Monaghan and th. Coy proceed to PUCHEVILLERS to take over billets.	

107 M G Coy
Vol 5

XXXVI

CONFIDENTIAL

War Diary of

107 Coy Machine Gun Corps

From 1st April to 29th April
1916

WAR DIARY or INTELLIGENCE SUMMARY

Army Form C. 2118.

Place	Date	Hour	Summary of Events and Information	Remarks and references to Appendices
Mailly Maillet	April 1st		Enemy quiet for last four days.	
	2nd		O.C. 87th M.G. Coy arrives and is shown round the trenches. 87th M.G. Coy arrive at 7.35 p.m.	
	3rd		Lieut Stewart and Marchi and five from 2nd Brown anderson 18 & a.	
			Second midman relieved by the 87th M.G. Coy.	
	4th		2nd Lieut Ruttan arrives from Quarters. Lieut Stewart Marchi and men will two orders proceed to Puchvillers hang an order in the truste.	
	5		Nearly the 93rd Inf Bde.	
	6th		Relief in 93rd Bde area relieved by 88th Rel M.G. Coy.	
	8th		Capt. Keyes and remaining orders proceed to Puchvillers.	
Puchvillers	7th		Company resting. Work in the morning and sports all in the afternoon.	
	8th			
	9th			
	10th			
	11th			

Army Form C. 2118.

WAR DIARY
or
INTELLIGENCE SUMMARY

(*Erase heading not required.*)

Instructions regarding War Diaries and Intelligence Summaries are contained in F. S. Regs., Part II. and the Staff Manual respectively. Title Pages will be prepared in manuscript.

Place	Date	Hour	Summary of Events and Information	Remarks and references to Appendices
Pucelmiller	April 13th			
	13th		Capt. Hogan attended conference of M.C. by Commander of the Division.	
	14th			
	15th			
	16th			
	17th		Capt. Hogan visited Hunter Staffs of Divn. Comm. Conference at Reb Hd.	
	18th			
	19th			
	20th			
Varennes	21st		Company moved to Varennes.	
	22nd			
	23rd			
	24th		Visit by Officer to enable of German trench opposite Thiepval Wood.	
	25th		Capt. Hogan visits trench Staffs of River Ancre. R.C.O's return round enemy German trench.	

Army Form C. 2118.

WAR DIARY
or
INTELLIGENCE SUMMARY
(Erase heading not required.)

Place	Date	Hour	Summary of Events and Information	Remarks and references to Appendices
Vaulx	April 25"			
	26"		Conference at Bat HQ	
	29"		Company go round and visit all German trenches and see where our own it is proposed to include strong points.	

MAYOTNE
107 M.G.C.
36
VOL 6.7

WAR DIARY or INTELLIGENCE SUMMARY

Army Form C.2118.

Place	Date	Hour	Summary of Events and Information	Remarks and references to Appendices
VARENNES	1.5.16		SERGT SMART & L/CPL CAMERON go on leave.	
	2			
	3			
	4			
	5			
	6		LT MONAGHAN returns from leave.	
	7		CAPT KEYSER goes on Paris leave.	
	8		Company relieves 109th Company in Thiepval Wood sector. Eight guns go into line. Two in front line & two in reserve dug-out. Remainder of Coy. in tents in MARTINSART WOOD. C & D Sections in line with Lieuts FRASER, MOORE, & ARTHUR.	
MARTINSART WOOD.	9		Two men from HAMMERHEAD SAP gun hut under arrest for leaving post.	
	10		Work on M.G. Emplacement in GEORGE STREET.	
	11		No 1 Gun moved from HAMMERHEAD SAP to junction of GEORGE STREET with front line. All quiet.	

Army Form C. 2118.

WAR DIARY
or
INTELLIGENCE SUMMARY

(Erase heading not required.)

Instructions regarding War Diaries and Intelligence Summaries are contained in F. S. Regs., Part II. and the Staff Manual respectively. Title Pages will be prepared in manuscript.

Place	Date	Hour	Summary of Events and Information	Remarks and references to Appendices
MARTINSART WOOD	12.5.16		All quiet on front. Work on Emplacements	
	13.5.16		Capt KEYSER returned from PARIS leave. Enemy use searchlight.	
	14.5.16		COURT MARTIAL on PTE THOMPSON & PTE BENSON for leaving posts. Found guilty and sentenced to 7 years P.S. Commuted by Brigadier to 2 years with H.L.	
			A+C Coys relieve B+D. Capt KEYSER + Lt SANDERSON.	
			Accumulator emplacement made for No 2 Gun. Bombardment at 12.45 pm on HAMEL SECTOR. All left from fired across river. 3 sto tunnel.	
	15.5.16			
	16.5.16		Enemy M.Gs active during night. French mortars fell near No 3 Gun. No damage done. Aeroplane flew over lines at 9.35 pm and threw out a red flare. Whether aircraft was friendly or hostile, not ascertained.	
	17.5.16		Dug-out near No.1 Gun completed & trench deepened. Emplacement made in mine S. of ELGIN AVENUE.	
	18.5.16		COURT MARTIAL on CORPL (ACTG SERGT) SMART. Sentenced to be reduced to ranks. Gun in Rue dispersed enemy patrol in DIAMOND WOOD. Hostile MGs and active. Hostile M.G. in Thiepval Chateau fired on (2,750 rounds) Lt MARTIN returned from leave & relieves CAPT KEYSER in trenches.	
	19.5.16		New emplacement made in JACK STREET. New emplacement begun 60 yards to left of No.2 gun called TOM FORT CASTLE	

WAR DIARY or INTELLIGENCE SUMMARY

Army Form C. 2118.

(Erase heading not required.)

Place	Date	Hour	Summary of Events and Information	Remarks and references to Appendices
MARTINSART WOOD	20.5.16		Night of No 6 begun. "Tom Fox's Castle" continued. Two search-lights played on our trenches. Enemy in JACK STREET trench working party in DIAMOND WOOD.	
	21.5.16		THIEPVAL WOOD heavily bombarded for about 5 minutes at midnight. Hostile M.Gs very active all night firing into our trenches with great accuracy.	
	22.5.16		Heavy Bombardment lasting about 1 hour apparently about MARY REDAN on north D it. Left guns fired 4000 rounds. Weather fine. Left guns fired some 4000 rounds into "Z" trench + BEAUCOURT.	
	23.5.16		Slight bombardment + bombing on right. Fires in THIEPVAL CEMETERY + BEAUCOURT STATION + trench. 2000 rounds.	
	24.5.16		Enemy M.G. active. Gun in rear to Rt of ELGIN AVENUE fired into new trench at enemy sentry in front of "Z" trench making him jump back into trench.	
	25.5.16		THIEPVAL CHATEAU. During day fired on fine trench Enemy's working party fired on in this new trench. Searchlight used by enemy. Alternative emplacement to No 4 gun started. 6000 rounds fired.	
	26.5.16		New enemy trench in Q.12.B.C.D. from Q.12.B9.3. to Q.12.C.4.3. Then turns to left to Q.12.C.5.2. and to Q.12.C.14. where it joins another trench from Q.12.D.5.4. to Q.12.C.5.2. in a fire trench. German working party in new trench fired on. 5200 rounds. Received case of gas attack.	
	27.5.16		Received in emplacements to keep belt boxes well above level of trench in case of gas attack.	

Place	Date	Hour	Summary of Events and Information	Remarks and references to Appendices
MARTINSART WOOD	28.5.16		Nothing to report	
	29.5.16		"	
	30.5.16		"	
	31.5.16		Fired on new trench at Q.12, B.C.D. 1300 rnds. No 5 Emplacement repaired & work continued on "TOM FOYS CASTLE."	

107th Brigade.
36th Division.

107th MACHINE GUN COMPANY

JUNE 1916:

Army Form C. 2118.

WAR DIARY or INTELLIGENCE SUMMARY
(Erase heading not required.)

Instructions regarding War Diaries and Intelligence Summaries are contained in F. S. Regs., Part II. and the Staff Manual respectively. Title Pages will be prepared in manuscript.

Place	Date	Hour	Summary of Events and Information	Remarks and references to Appendices
MARTINSART WOOD	1/8/16		Fired 61/2 Trench number of rounds fired 1100. Communication trench leading to no. 6 gun position built up, also one of the reserve guns fired into THIEVAL in order to mark the mean point of the village.	
	2/8/16		A hut, which seemed the made of corrugated iron, located at the point where the new tram to R.19 B&D goes the enemy's third line, was fired upon 1300 rounds used. Puffs at cement implements made at no. 1 gun.	
	3/8/16		Batt'n sides active with artillery on our left and night bombardment. Lasting ends of two hours. Enemy trench Mortars very active on night sector.	
	4/8/16		Artillery activity on our night bombardment lasting two hours. Trench Mortars fall very near 6R 3 gun.	
	5/8/16		At 11.0 P.M. our artillery started a bombardment of the enemy's lines previous to a raid being made from the left Sub-section until the ceap in 62.18.c. Our plans of co-operation was as follows:- no 2 gun to traverse enemy front line in R.19 b. no 5 gun fire on communication trench R.7.0.0.2., no.6 gun on front line in R.28. no.1 gun on artillery opened fire the enemy opened a heavy bombardment on the THIEPVAL WOOD and sector using heavy shells and trench mortars, our 3 gun had to leave the open implacement for the cover in 46.5 which was also an auxiliary implacement had to stop firing owing to shrapnel and heavy shells falling R.Gardener and L.tengill anyway got killed.	

Army Form C.2118.

WAR DIARY
or
INTELLIGENCE SUMMARY
(Erase heading not required.)

Instructions regarding War Diaries and Intelligence Summaries are contained in F.S. Regs., Part II. and the Staff Manual respectively. Title Pages will be prepared in manuscript.

Place	Date	Hour	Summary of Events and Information	Remarks and references to Appendices
	5/6/16		No 6 gun fired 950 rounds although heavy shell were landing all round. The entrance to the Emplacement was broken down, the emplacement being an open one. B and D sections relieved A and C sections in the line. No 5 gun fired 1000 rounds the	
	6/6/16		BEAUCOURT. Quiet.	
	7/6/16		Stones for concrete emplacement taken up and dumped in front line. Nos 3 & 5 guns fired 250 rounds during the night.	
	9/6/16		Arrange for concrete emplacement Hyperides during the night. Enemy Machine guns very active. No 4 gun fired 750 rounds on GRANDCOURT–THIEPVAL ROAD. No 5 gun fired 550 rounds on trenches between Z and REDAN. Capt Skeyas goes on leave and 2/Lt Smith No 50 gun to Company for duty.	
	10/6/16		Enemy rifle fired on Louis to a very heavy bombardment between 11.30 A.m. and 1.0 m. No 5 gun. Haphazardly put out of action. No 5 gun bought up and mounted in No 5 emplacement. Lieut I. Wilson and Private Mosleyarash killed whilst firing the gun, the remainder of the Section wounded at 6 pm. Nos 6 & 5 Section proceeds to down and Barrow Lane billets whilst carrying ammunition to the gun. Parties to the new emplacements	
	11/6/16		was being carried out on the new emplacements.	
	12/6/16		Work on the concrete emplacement continued.	
	13/6/16		Enemy Machine guns active, we is concentrates on the new emplacements and no work could be started. All guns found dug in new No 5 Emplacement and work continued at 2/Lt S.C. Lyef.	

2449 Wt. W14957/M90 750,000 1/16 J.B.C. & A. Forms/C.2118/12.

WAR DIARY or INTELLIGENCE SUMMARY

Army Form C.2118.

Instructions regarding War Diaries and Intelligence Summaries are contained in F. S. Regs., Part II. and the Staff Manual respectively. Title Pages will be prepared in manuscript.

(Erase heading not required.)

Place	Date	Hour	Summary of Events and Information	Remarks and references to Appendices
	14/6/16		Enemy very active with trench mortars, two mortars fell in no 1 gun position and killed 2/Lieut. Molloch and four others. The trench was watched and nothing was found of the gun. The sandbagging of the new position at M.9h was carried out, also work at 9.4.5. Machine guns & Artillery firing active. SBS's men have put in and hole dug for no 6 position	
	15/6/16		Quiet. no 6 new emplacement put in and work continued on M.9.6. and 9.4.5 emplacements. Firing nil. Recently 9/6 band cases returns from leave.	
	16/6/16		Nothing to report.	
	17/6/16		Nothing to report. B and D Lieuts. & Lieut A and C.	
	18/6/16		Nothing to report.	
	19/6/16		Nothing to report.	
	20/6/16		Nothing to report.	
	21/6/16		Nothing to report. Lieut Hagen returns from leave	
	22/6/16		Nothing to report.	
	23/6/16		Nothing to report. A sections relieves B and my 9/Lieut also Lieut D. Cochrane Lieut G.F.B. G. Boyer HAMEL.	
	24/6/16		Our artillery shell all the enemy wire and trenches, Machine guns fire 3500 rds on the enemy wire.	
	25/6/16		Our artillery and trench mortars subjected enemys trenches to a very heavy bombardment. Bombardment continues POZIERES and OVILLERS observed on fire. Our no 6 position also in SLutjt Otto Alliak being wounded, no 2 position also being badly damaged.	

2449 Wt. W4957/M90 750,000 1/16 J.B.C. & A. Forms/C.2118/12.

Army Form C. 2118.

WAR DIARY
or
INTELLIGENCE SUMMARY
(Erase heading not required.)

Instructions regarding War Diaries and Intelligence Summaries are contained in F. S. Regs., Part II. and the Staff Manual respectively. Title Pages will be prepared in manuscript.

Place	Date	Hour	Summary of Events and Information	Remarks and references to Appendices
	27/6/16		Between 3.30 and 4.30 p.m. our toungrines fired 40 gas cylinders fired on the enemy with 130 rounds. The enemy shell the front line and THIEPVAL WOOD and very heavy shells.	
	27/6/16		The bombardment of the enemys trenches continues. Our guns fire on the wire.	
	28/6/16		The bombardment continues. The enemys emplacement being blown up by the trench shells.	
	29/6/16		The bombardment continued, especially intense by our artillery.	
	30/6/16		The bombardment continued.	
	31/6/16		The bombardment continued.	

2449 Wt. W14957/M90 750,000 1/16 J.B.C. & A. Forms/C.2118/12.

107th Brigade.
36th Division.

107th BRIGADE MACHINE GUN COMPANY

JULY 1916

C O N F I D E N T I A L.	36th. Division G. S. 292

D. A. G.,
  G. H. Q.,
    3rd. Echelon.

        With reference to your memo. of 20th instant., herewith War Diary of 107th Brigade Machine Gun Company.
        The delay in rendering this is regretted, but it was understood that it had been forwarded direct to you.
        There appears to have been some misunderstanding with regard to Diaries from Trench Mortar Batteries. Both Divisional Artillery and Infantry Brigades state that these have not previously been called for, and the 108th Brigade state that while their Stokes Battery was temporarily attached to another Division its Diary was returned from the Base with an intimation that it was not required.
        Arrangements have, however, now been made to ensure that the instructions contained in War Office letter 121/8569(M.O.1) of 28/6/16 are strictly carried out in future, and the Diaries of all units of the Division will be despatched to you from this office on the third of each month.

29/8/16.

                            MAJOR-GENERAL.
        COMMANDING 36TH. (ULSTER) DIVISION.

36/ July
107 M.G.C.
36th (Ulster) Division
Vol. 8

Army Form C. 2118.

WAR DIARY
or
INTELLIGENCE SUMMARY
(Erase heading not required.)

Place	Date	Hour	Summary of Events and Information	Remarks and references to Appendices
	July 1	7.30 am	The guns of the 107th Coy. M.G. Corps took part in the attack made by the 36th (Ulster) Division. The guns were attached to the 107th Brigade in the following manner:- A section four guns in THIEPVAL WOOD to support attack on right bank of the river ANCRE. As soon as they had finished this support they were to follow the 8th R.Ir.Rif. in the attack. These guns were under the command of Lieut Stewart. B Section 2 guns under Lieut Sanderson with the 9th R.Ir.Rif.; 2 guns under Lieut Murray Ken with the 15th R.Ir.Rif. C Section under 2nd Lieut Martin supported the attack on the left bank of the river ANCRE from the HAMEL subsector and then were brought into Brigade reserve in THIEPVAL WOOD D Section 2 guns under Lieut Fraser with the 10th R.Ir.Rifles; 2 guns under 2nd Lieut Gee with the 8th R.Ir.Rif. The Company's casualties were as follows:- Lieut Sanderson killed also 4 O.R. Lieut Monaghan, Lieut Kriger, 2nd Lieut Gee, and 18 O.R. wounded. 5 O.R. missing	
	July 2	2.0pm	C Section 2 guns under 2nd Lieut Martin accompanied the composite battalion of the 107th Brigade in the attack on the German front line trenches on the left of THIEPVAL VILLAGE 2nd Lieut Martin and 1 O.R. were wounded in the German trenches 8 guns of the Company were lost in the attack.	

Army Form C. 2118.

107 Machine Gun Corps

WAR DIARY
or
INTELLIGENCE SUMMARY
(Erase heading not required.)

Instructions regarding War Diaries and Intelligence Summaries are contained in F.S. Regs., Part II. and the Staff Manual respectively. Title Pages will be prepared in manuscript.

Place	Date	Hour	Summary of Events and Information	Remarks and references to Appendices
	2/7/16	9.0 p.m	The Company moved from THIEPVAL WOOD to billets in MARTINSART	
	3/7/16		In Billets	
	4/7/16		Moved to HARPONVILLE	
	5/7/16		Moved to RUBEMPRÉ	
	6/7/16		Parades.	
	7/7/16		" 2nd Lieut A.W. Atkins and 2nd Lieut J.H. Robson reported for duty also a draft of 200R	
	8/7/16		" 2nd Lieut A. Dent-Young with a draft of 14 O.R. reported for duty.	
	9/7/16		" Capt. A.G. Keyser C.O. of the Company reported sick and was detained in Hospital	
	10/7/16		Moved to BERNAVILLE	
	11/7/16		Marched to AUXI LE CHATEAU and entrained for THIENNES detrained there + marched to	
	12/7/16		WORDRECQUES	
			2nd Lieut H.C. Lyon and 2nd Lieut J. Barker reported for duty; 2nd Lieut Barker reported sick and was detained in Hospital	
	13/7/16		Marched to WESTROVE	
	14/7/16		Parades as per programme.	
	15/7/16		Parades as per programme.	
	16/7/16		Parades as per programme.	
	17/7/16		Parades as per programme.	

Army Form C. 2118.

167 MG Coy

WAR DIARY
or
INTELLIGENCE SUMMARY
(Erase heading not required.)

Instructions regarding War Diaries and Intelligence Summaries are contained in F. S. Regs., Part II. and the Staff Manual respectively. Title Pages will be prepared in manuscript.

Place	Date	Hour	Summary of Events and Information	Remarks and references to Appendices
	18/7/16		Parades as per programme	
	19/7/16		Parades as per programme	
	20/7/16		Marched to BOLLEZEELE	
	21/7/16		Marched to ROOSENDAEL	
	22/7/16		Marched to LONG. CROIX in the HONDEGHEM area	
	23/7/16		Marched to STEENWERK	
	24/7/16		Parades as per programme	
	25/7/16		Parades as per programme	
	26/7/16		Parades as per programme	
	27/7/16		Parades as per programme	
	28/7/16		Marched to KORTEPYP	
	29/7/16		Parades	
	30/7/16		Parades	
	31/7/16		Parades. Officers N.C.O.s and men visit the trenches with a view to taking over from the 108th M.G. Company.	

R.W. Falkes Capt
L. M. gun Coy

Comdg 107 MG Coy

Army Form C.2118.

Vol 9

107th Coy M.G. Corps

WAR DIARY
or
INTELLIGENCE SUMMARY

(Erase heading not required.)

Instructions regarding War Diaries and Intelligence Summaries are contained in F.S. Regs., Part II. and the Staff Manual respectively. Title Pages will be prepared in manuscript.

Place	Date	Hour	Summary of Events and Information	Remarks and references to Appendices
BULFORD CAMP	1/8/16		B & D section relieved the P gun of the 108th Coy M.G. Corps in the line. Enemy machine guns were fairly active.	
	2/8/16		The enemy shelled the L.O.P. 5 limited fire was obtained no replacement, & A & C men stores in. There was no casualties	
	3/8/16		Orders were received that another gun in the line A & C section was relieved	
	4/8/16		A & C section Came out of the line	
	5/8/16		A & C section took over from 109th Coy M.G. Corps in the line. B & D were relieved by the 108th Coy M.G. Corps.	
	6/8/16		Enemy shelled gun line, however troths with batched numbers	
	7/8/16		New machine gun emplacement made.	
	8/8/16		The Enemy bombarded the front line but no damage was done. The division for front is NORTH MIDLAND in strength.	

WAR DIARY
or
INTELLIGENCE SUMMARY

(Erase heading not required.)

Army Form C. 2118.

107th Bde M.G. Corps

Place	Date	Hour	Summary of Events and Information	Remarks and references to Appendices
	9/8/16		A new s/ph position has been at N.36.C.8.15 & 2 August at N.36.C.6.5.45.	PLOEGSTEERT 28 S.W. 4 Edition 3.D / Trenches
	10/8/16		A Vickers gun & two emplacements at N.36.C.8.5.3	
	11/8/16		Work was continued on the day and the wood myth was done.	
	12/8/16		Work was continued on the day nor. The enemy was very quiet.	
	13/8/16		B+D section relieved A+C in the line	
	14/8/16		The Enemy has shelled ct SOUVENIR FARM & the trenches & wire for our carriers and on HELL FARM & BIRTHDAY FARM.	
	15/8/16		Enemy machine guns have active during the night.	
	16/8/16		The enemy shelled WULVERGHEM CHURCH, BONE POINT & BIRTHDAY FARM has fired on	
	17/8/16		BONE POINT has again been on Enemy machine guns have very active	
	18/8/16		About 2.30 pm a gas alarm was turned on the left of our brigade but no gas was detected.	

Army Form C. 2118.

WAR DIARY
or
INTELLIGENCE SUMMARY
(Erase heading not required.)

107th. Coy. M.G. Corps.

Instructions regarding War Diaries and Intelligence Summaries are contained in F.S. Regs., Part II. and the Staff Manual respectively. Title Pages will be prepared in manuscript.

Place	Date	Hour	Summary of Events and Information	Remarks and references to Appendices
	19/8/16		Enemy bombarded our front line & support trenches for about an hour & a half. Smell shrapnel fire on the enemy near + front trenches.	PLOEGSTEERT 28SW4.Ed.3D Trones
	20/8/16		Work in company not & to new spots in advance of N.36.C.85.3	
	21/8/16		Attended B.H.D. [unclear] M. Trenches	
	22/8/16		Relieved 3½ + 4 p.m. Plans to transmitted to Colony + D.N. advising on both sides of the old headers from fire line past entire dump to [unclear] lower the [unclear]	
	23/8/16		Moved from headers from 3½ to 5 p.m. with artillery + hired hunters. Called W.D.2 By the foot gun, [unclear] to command the fire from the support [unclear] [unclear] on known as the M. James lane & utterfield & entry to every [unclear] from about N36.a.70.25 down to the shared offensive near tip of M½.	
	24/8/16		Enemy machine guns were very quiet. 3½ to 4 p.m. Enemy [unclear] fire again turned up from in the new line at T.1 to 90.85. The enemy flattens the ground to Dugevine [unclear] along the [unclear]	

WAR DIARY
or
INTELLIGENCE SUMMARY
(Erase heading not required.)

Army Form C. 2118.

107 R Coy M.G.C.

Place	Date	Hour	Summary of Events and Information	Remarks and references to Appendices
	25/8/16		There has very little machine gun fire. The enemy artillery shown [illegible] did not [illegible] [illegible] the 28th [illegible] at the depot in relief.	PLOEGSTEERT 28 W. & 3 D /1000
	26/8/16		Enemy machine guns have been telling our fatigue parties. One machine gun was [illegible] active during the night firing on [illegible] roads. I think taking the enemy [illegible] gun at Pt 85 map left E. Bill [illegible] at Pt 33 G I N.E.C. About 10.30 pm 200 rounds were fired on enemy wiring party at T 6 1 80 95.	
	27/8/16		Our M.G. firing [illegible] fire at 6am & 9am at 6 lily 4/25 at enemy wiring at [illegible] & rear M Ct. 11.30 fire with 2 guns MG. 1 shrapnel at Pt MC left [illegible] 2 Rd 84. Both the German front lines were moved up into the front line at night. The left gun fired about 1500 rounds & so kept up the enemy to [illegible] the placements fire.	
	28/8/16		[illegible] any retaliation. 1 O.R. Kr. Kramer dry hacksaw.	
	29/8/16		27 [illegible] 308 C. pte. B. Kramer dry hacksaw on front to the trenches. B+D rection relieve A+C & M.T. trench	

Army Form C. 2118.

WAR DIARY
or
INTELLIGENCE SUMMARY
(Erase heading not required.)

107th Coy. M.G.C.

Place	Date	Hour	Summary of Events and Information	Remarks and references to Appendices
	2/9/16		Shewlow the enemy Y[illegible] Point North bombarded the trench point jones nights. Indirect fire was opened at on THE HOSPICE.	
	3/9/16		Our artillery shewed fire for 1/2 an hour from 1.30 am. The enemy reflect slightly with trench mortar. Indirect fire was opened out on the HOSPICE & GER1 village.	

M[illegible]
Capt
107th Coy. M.G.C.

VOL 10

WAR DIARY
or
INTELLIGENCE SUMMARY
(Erase heading not required.)

Army Form C. 2118.

107th Coy M.G. Corps

Place	Date	Hour	Summary of Events and Information	Remarks and references to Appendices
	1/9/16		All was quiet up till 1.30 a.m. when the two little attacks were launched by a heavy barrage down two draws. 2000 rounds were fired during the night at enemy communication trench & cross road behind the enemy line.	
	2/9/16		All was quiet except at 5.20 p.m. when enemy bombarded STONETREMBIR with trench mortars. 1500 rounds were fired at enemy communication trench. 9pts J.L. Luther rejoined the Coy from hosp. for his first time.	
	3/9/16		At 11 p.m. the alarm was received from the Inf. & troops stood to due to the enemy attack. Till 11.45 p.m. no fire was experienced. The enemy communicat'n trench & cross roads were fired at intervals during the night.	Our artillery opened
	4/9/16		The night was exceptionally quiet. A little firing was done on the enemy front & comm'n lines.	
	5/9/16		B & D sections have relieved in the trenches by A+C.	

Army Form C. 2118.

WAR DIARY
or
INTELLIGENCE SUMMARY
(Erase heading not required.)

107th Coy. M.G. Corps.

Instructions regarding War Diaries and Intelligence Summaries are contained in F.S. Regs., Part II. and the Staff Manual respectively. Title Pages will be prepared in manuscript.

Place	Date	Hour	Summary of Events and Information	Remarks and references to Appendices
	6/9/16		Our artillery opened fire at 10 pm + continued for two hours. The enemy reply was inexpensive.	PLOEGSTEERT 28 SW Edn. 3D /corr
	7/9/16		Our artillery was very active throughout day & night. No firing of any importance was done.	
	8/9/16		Our artillery was again active. The enemy dropped some shells in the direct of SOUVENIR FARM. Two round in front of L'ENFER FM.	
	9/9/16		Gas alarm was raised at 8.45 pm. Every body stood to arms but no signs of gas experienced. The enemy commenced shells in front at intervals during the night.	
	10/9/16		The night was quiet except for our own and the enemy's artillery at 11 pm. Some rifle in front of the enemy front. Rifle & machine gun fire. There was a considerable amount of enemy machine gun activity from today's	
	11/9/16		All p.m.	
	12/9/16		A artillery shoot was to have been carried out between 4 pm & 4.30 pm. 14,000 rounds were to have been fired at the high ground behind light railway etc.	

WAR DIARY
or
INTELLIGENCE SUMMARY
(Erase heading not required.)

Army Form C. 2118.

107 M. Coy. M. G. Corps.

Place	Date	Hour	Summary of Events and Information	Remarks and references to Appendices
	12/9/16 (contd)		in the enemy lines.	
	13/9/16		The night was quiet except for machine gun fire from our men. The night at various points taking the enemy lines. All relieving the B.E.D. in the trenches.	
	14/9/16		Our artillery was active throughout the day & night. 9 guns were in front in the enemy saps for communication trench onwards. 3 more are gone during the night at various points in the enemy lines.	
	15/9/16			
	16/9/16		Our artillery did two short shoots during the day, one in the morning & the other in the afternoon. Two more guns forward in various points in the enemy lines including the Starch Factory at U.2.a.85.05 which was reported to 7th Corps circular. We were then unable to counter-attack. Relieve the guns at E.28.a.m.	

Army Form C. 2118.

WAR DIARY
or
INTELLIGENCE SUMMARY
(Erase heading not required.)

107 Inf. Bry. M.G. Coy.

Instructions regarding War Diaries and Intelligence Summaries are contained in F. S. Regs., Part II. and the Staff Manual respectively. Title Pages will be prepared in manuscript.

Place	Date	Hour	Summary of Events and Information	Remarks and references to Appendices
	18/9/16		Our Artillery opened a tremendousness at 12.15pm which lasted two hours. The enemy front in front of K. Was strafed with DIAGONAL.	PLOEGSTEERT 28 SW Edn 3 1/10,000
		10.00	Men fired on K Track tramway (W1 & 80.05)	
		3.00	on K. tramway track in K vicinity of Bone Pt	
		11.00	on H. MENIN ES RD	
	19/9/16	7.000	Normal rounds fired during the night. morning fairly quiet. 2/Lt J. Parker, 1 N.C.O. & 28 O.Rs arrived by from Bou.	
		6.00	Normal ne fire of enemy front in the enemy line. Inter Much firing fairly active in reply.	
	20/9/16		No firing of any importance done during the day from here. the enemy fairly quiet.	
	21/9/16	10.00	Men finished BONE PT.	
		3.000	- - - NYLYERGHEM-WYTSCHAETE RD	
		1.50	- - - O.25.a.	
		12.00	- - - SLOPING ROOF FM & BIRTHDAY FM	

Army Form C. 2118.

WAR DIARY
or
INTELLIGENCE SUMMARY
(Erase heading not required.)

107th Cdn M G Coy

Place	Date	Hour	Summary of Events and Information	Remarks and references to Appendices
	22/9/16		Our artillery [opened ?] March was very active between 3 & 4 pm. Our heavies shelled ONTARIO FM at 4.15 pm	ROEGSTEERT ROSES Edition 3 10,000
	23/9/16	8.00	Nth we fired in enfilade fire at enemy line	
	24/9/16		Intensive attack being [carried ?] at K Bruce 3 running V.2.a. 80-05	
		6 am 17 am	there were heavy enemy barrage [inside ?] 2nd [Moreles ?]	
		5000 Nth we fired at enemy front below the enemy line		
	25/9/16		The fire from LEFT PINKIE has moved up 150 [yards ?] from line as the regained B Coy 10th R 9 Rifle [were ?] who were very [busy ?]	
			6000 Rds were fired at various points especially V.2.a. 80-05	
	26/9/16	15.00	Rds were fired on BONE PT	
		10.00	- - M. man O.25.c	
		10.00	- - MESSINES RD	
		10.00	- - HELL FM	

Army Form C. 2118.

107th Coy M.G. Corps

WAR DIARY
or
INTELLIGENCE SUMMARY
(Erase heading not required.)

Place	Date	Hour	Summary of Events and Information	Remarks and references to Appendices
PLOEGSTEERT	27/9/16		0600 Oth were firing on roads, kept communication trenches in the enemy lines.	Refer to Appendix 3 for map.
	28/9/16		B & D relieved A & C returns to H. Encls. 4000 Rds has been fired during the night. Rain & foggy forenoon & evening fine.	
	29/9/16		There is no landmark around Irish M.N.E. which is the afternoon. No special firing has been reply save the trainer firing.	
	30/9/16		1250 rounds were fired at O.31.d.0-60.	
		2250	- - - -	SLOPING ROOF FARM; BIRTHDAY F.M.
		1710	- - - -	crossroad O.32.d.

R.M. Forde
Capt.

O/o 107th Inf. Bde.

Herewith please find War Diary for month of October 1916.

R M Forbes
Capt
1/11/16   107th Coy M.G.C.

Army Form C. 2118.

Vol II

107 Coy M.G. Corps

WAR DIARY
or
INTELLIGENCE SUMMARY
(Erase heading not required.)

Place	Date	Hour	Summary of Events and Information	Remarks and references to Appendices
PLOEGSTEERT 28 S.W. Ed.3 1/10000	1/10/16		Enemy Trench Mortars very active between 11.30 pm + 12 mid-night. 6000 rounds fired during the night at various points.	
	2/10/16		Weather conditions very bad. Trench Mortar activity on both sides. 6000 rounds fired on enemy strong points + support trenches.	
	3/10/16		B + D sections relieved by A + C sections. 5000 rounds fired during night mainly on traversing fire on enemy roads.	
	4/10/16		Enemy Artillery + Trench Mortars bombarded our front line between 8 pm + 9.30 pm. Our Artillery replied. 3000 rounds fired on enemy communication trenches + roads during bombardment. Our M.Gs very active during night. 12,000 rounds fired from 8 guns at enemy's front line, support trenche + strong points.	
	5/10/16		Quiet night. Little Machine Gun fire. Enemy used search-light during night.	
	6/10/16		Our Artillery active throughout the night. 5000 rounds fired at various points behind Enemy line.	

Army Form C. 2118.

WAR DIARY
or
INTELLIGENCE SUMMARY
(Erase heading not required.)

104th Coy M.G. Corps

Place	Date	Hour	Summary of Events and Information	Remarks and references to Appendices
PLOEGSTEERT 28 S.W. E & 3	8/10/16		Quiet night. Our Artillery fairly active registering throughout day. Usual M.G. fire	
	9/10/16		Gas sent over from our lines at 1.30 a.m. Artillery bombarded at 1.34 aided by Trench Mortars. During this time our M.Gs very active. 10000 rounds fired from 6 guns at enemy communication trenches & front line.	/10 000
	10/10/16		Quiet night. 5000 rounds fired at enemy roads + communication trenches. Artillery + trench mortar registration on both sides.	
	11/10/16		4000 rounds fired in vicinity of 4 HUNS FARM, MESSINES + RDS + BIRTHDAY FARM.	
	12/10/16		Intensive bombardment by enemy our Artillery + Trench Mortars on enemy front line. This was followed by a raiding party. Enemy threw up a number of red flares + then green + white ones. Our M.Gs active during bombardment.	
	13/10/16		Enemy opened heavy bombardment of trench mortars at 2.30 p.m. This was maintained for about an hour at intervals.	

Army Form C. 2118.

WAR DIARY
or
INTELLIGENCE SUMMARY
(Erase heading not required.)

107th Coy. M. E. Coys.

Instructions regarding War Diaries and Intelligence Summaries are contained in F.S. Regs., Part II. and the Staff Manual respectively. Title Pages will be prepared in manuscript.

Place	Date	Hour	Summary of Events and Information	Remarks and references to Appendices
PLOEGSTEERT	14/10/16		The enemy activity has increased slightly. Talk by day snipers in various targets within the enemy line to our front. 4000 rounds were fired at various targets within the enemy line	28.Div Ed. 3 /10.0.0
	15/10/16		At TC section relieve B.1.D. in the trenches. 1000 rounds were fired at the MESSINES ROAD — L'ENFER FARM. 1000	
	16/10/16		The enemy machine guns were less active than usual during the night. At 4 pm our Trench mortars rattlely opened a bombardment on the enemy front line & support lines but no trace of enemy's reply was found. No change in the enemy made remarkable trench.	
	17/10/16		Enemy machine guns were fairly active. We again bombarded the enemy front line from 4 pm – 7 pm.	
	18/10/16		Our artillery fired more than usual during the night. 2000 rounds were fired during the night at the enemy front line opposite	
	19/10/16		Enemy aeroplane came over line at 5 pm. 1000 rounds were fired at enemy front at SLOPING ROOF FM. 1000 at PETITE PUITS & 1000 rounds at enemy front line	

Army Form C. 2118.

WAR DIARY
or
INTELLIGENCE SUMMARY
(Erase heading not required.)

107th Coy. M. E. Corps.

Place	Date	Hour	Summary of Events and Information	Remarks and references to Appendices
PLOEGSTEERT	20/09/16		Hostile machine gun was fairly active throughout the night. 7000 rounds were fired on road, communication trench, dump & lately the enemy line.	26.hrs. Gd 3 / 10000
	21/09/16		BTD. section relieved Coy. to the head. 5000 rounds were fired at various points in enemy line.	
	22/09/16		A searchlight was noticed in the district of MESSINES. 9 camps & new store lines. One Lewis & Mortar bombarded the enemy line at 2.30pm. 12.50 rounds fired on SLOPING ROOF Fm. 1000 " " " NULVERGHEM – WYTSCHAETE ROAD 1000 " " trench LTR left of SLOPING ROOF Fm.	
	23/09/16		Exceptionally quiet during the hours of daylight no again observed. 3500 rounds were fired at various points with enemy line.	
	24/09/16		Cts. 2, 3. hrs. There was considerable trench mortar & artillery activity on both sides 4000 rounds were fired during the night on roads & communication lines in the enemy line.	

2449 Wt. W14957/M90 750,000 1/16 J.B.C. & A. Forms/C.2118/12.

WAR DIARY or INTELLIGENCE SUMMARY

Army Form C. 2118.

107th Coy. M. G. Corps

Place	Date	Hour	Summary of Events and Information	Remarks and references to Appendices
	25/9/16		At 3 p.m. the enemy attacked trenches occupied on left side. Our Artillery fired on the line to drive. At 3.40 the enemy sent up several red + white flares.	PLOEGSTEERT RSSW Sh 3 1/10000
	26/9/16		12.50 rounds were fired on WULVERGHEM - MESSINES RD 12.50 - - - - BIRTHDAY FM & SLOPING ROOF FM. Enemy aeroplane very low and just over the wire. At 11 A.M. an hostile aeroplane dropped 3 enemy birds in the vicinity of ONTARIO FM. 3000 rounds were fired on various points in the enemy line.	
	27/9/16		At C Section relieved B & D in the trenches. 5000 rounds were fired on various points in the enemy line.	
	28/9/16		Hostile machine gun swept the MESSINES road from 10 pm - 11pm. 1000 rounds were fired on MESSINES ROAD, 1000 rounds at L'ENFER FM, 1000 rounds at BIRTHDAY FM.	
	29/9/16		Enemy M gs have been active the whole during the night. Our fire was on various enemy M.G.s + communication trs.	

WAR DIARY
or
INTELLIGENCE SUMMARY

(Erase heading not required.)

107th Coy M.G. Corps

Army Form C. 2118.

Place	Date	Hour	Summary of Events and Information	Remarks and references to Appendices
	30/10/16		2000 rounds were fired at BIRTH DAY FM	PLOEGSTEERT 28 SW E1 & 3 /10000
			2000 " " " SLOPING ROOF FM	
			1000 " " " MESSINES RD	
	31/10/16		Enemy shelled N. MIDLAND FM from 3 pm - 4 pm have never been found at work. ammunition & I know him.	

N.P. Poole
Capt.
107th Coy M.G.C.

Army Form C. 2118.

WAR DIARY or INTELLIGENCE SUMMARY

107th Coy. M.G.C. Vol 12

(Erase heading not required.)

Instructions regarding War Diaries and Intelligence Summaries are contained in F. S. Regs., Part II. and the Staff Manual respectively. Title Pages will be prepared in manuscript.

Place	Date	Hour	Summary of Events and Information	Remarks and references to Appendices
BULFORD CAMP	1.11.16		Our Artillery + Trench Mortars bombarded enemy trenches at 2 pm. Enemy replied heavily. Enemy searchlights in operation at 7 pm.	PLOEGSTEERT 28 S.W. Ed 3 1/10,000
	2.11.16		Enemy M.G. & rifle fire more active than usual. Fired upon enemy patrol located in NOMANSLAND at 10 pm. B + D. Section relieved A + C.	
	3.11.16		Our Trench Mortars active during afternoon. Small retaliation. Our M.Gs active chiefly in traversing enemy roads.	
	4.11.16		We dispersed a working party at O31.b. 3.0.8.5. with our M.G. fire at 2.45 pm. Our guns fired at intervals through the night at strong point behind German line.	
	5.11.16		Enemy shelled the LOOP during the night. Enemy searchlights observed from direction of MESSINES. Fired at intervals during the night at points known to be occupied - chiefly as 4 HUNS FARM & BIRTHDAY FARM.	
	6.11.16		9 pm a few small shells fell near O14 GONAL Pos 2. Inland bombardment on our left at 10 pm. A large fire observed north of MESSINES at 11 pm. Usual programme of fire on enemy communication trenches & strong points.	
	7.11.16		Enemy bombed his wire throughout night, otherwise all quiet. Fired at intervals during night some 4000 rounds - Target:- BIRTHDAY FARM. WULVERGHEM - WYTSCHAETE ROAD.	

WAR DIARY or INTELLIGENCE SUMMARY

Army Form C. 2118.

107th. Coy. M.G.C.

Place	Date	Hour	Summary of Events and Information	Remarks and references to Appendices
	8.11.16		Machine Guns BIRTHDAY FARM & MESSINES ROAD fired on at intervals. Enemy used search light at 9 pm & sent up two large spray rockets.	
	9.11.16		A & C sections relieved B & D. Enemy roads harassed during night.	
	10.11.16		Enemy aeroplane over our lines at 9.30 pm, dropped white & green lights. SLOPING ROOF FARM – HELL FARM – BIRTHDAY FARM & roads near there points fired on.	
	11.11.16		We fired on various points on MESSINES hillside. Enemy replied actively.	
	12.11.16		Enemy M.G.s very active. We again bombed his wire. Our guns also very active during night.	
	13.11.16		Enemy artillery active throughout day – also Trench Mortars at 10.30 am. Fired 5000 rounds at enemy strong points.	
	14.11.16		Our artillery, Trench Mortars & M.G.s fired on enemy lines between 11.30 & 12.30 am. Enemy's reply weak.	
	15.11.16		Enemy M.G.s too active. Fired 4000 rounds at enemy road & communication trenches.	

WAR DIARY or INTELLIGENCE SUMMARY

Army Form C. 2118.

107th Coy M.G.C.

Place	Date	Hour	Summary of Events and Information	Remarks and references to Appendices
	16.11.16		At 10 pm in response to a red & green flare our artillery opened an intense bombardment on our left for one hour. Enemy artillery active throughout day. Our H.Q.s active though night.	
	17.11.16		Little activity on either side.	
	18.11.16		Enemy were searchlight at 7 pm. Enemy bombarded our left sector with trench mortars and artillery at 2.15 am. Our artillery, trench mortars & H.G.s replied vigorously.	
	19.11.16		Usual programme of fire carried out. Targets included BIRTHDAY FARM, SLOPING ROOF FARM & L'ENFER WOOD.	
	20.11.16		Our gun at SHELL FARM put out of action by shell passing through loophole. Shell did not explode. No casualties.	
	21.11.16		Relief took place. Enemy transport roads harassed with fire at frequent intervals. Weather conditions bad. Little activity on either side.	
	23.11.16		Enemy Machine guns very active, especially at 6.30 pm. Red lights sent up. No apparent cause.	

Army Form C. 2118.

WAR DIARY
or
INTELLIGENCE SUMMARY
(Erase heading not required.)

107A Coy M.G.C.

Place	Date	Hour	Summary of Events and Information	Remarks and references to Appendices
	24.11.16		Unusual artillery activity during day, particularly between 2 & 3 p.m. Field 8000 rounds at enemy strong points during night.	
	25.11.16		Very little activity on either side. M.Gs traversed enemy roads between MESSINES and WYTSCHAETE.	
	26.11.16		Heavy Mist prevailed - Quiet day & night. 1500 rounds fired in vicinity of BIRTHDAY FARM and SLOPING ROOF FARM.	
	27.11.16		Heavy Mist again. No artillery or aerial activity. Transport heard on MESSINES - WYTSCHAETE ROAD at 2am.	
	28.11.16		Trench mortar bombardment on our left at 2.45 p.m. Enemy M.Gs active at 5.30 p.m. but afterwards quiet during the night.	
	29.11.16		Very small activity all day in consequence of heavy mist.	
	30.11.16		Intense bombardment of enemy trenches by our trench mortars at 2 p.m. Enemy retaliated about 3 p.m. but only slightly. During the bombardment our M.Gs fired some 2000 rounds at enemy communications.	

W.Barker
Capt.

Army Form C. 2118.

WAR DIARY
or
INTELLIGENCE SUMMARY

(Erase heading not required.)

107th Coy. M.G. Corps.

Place	Date	Hour	Summary of Events and Information	Remarks and references to Appendices
	1.12.16		2000 rounds fired on following targets - L'ENFER - 4 HUNS FM, BIRTHDAY FM and HELL FM.	
	2.12.16		Relief day. 3000 rounds fired on enemy strong points + C.Ts.	
	3.12.16		Artillery activity. Several shells fell near NORTHUMBERLAND ROAD for without damaging emplacement. 3000 rounds on FOUR HUNS FARM, HOSPICE, L'ENFER WOOD.	
	4.12.16		Traversed the MESSINES - WYTSCHAETE RD + roads leading to HOSPICE + 4 HUNS FM 5000 rounds.	
	5.12.16		MESSINES - WULVERGHEM RD + HILL below MESSINES traversed. Enemy parapets swept during night. 3500 rounds.	
	6.12.16		3000 rounds on HOSPICE, SLOPING ROOF FM, L'ENFER WOOD + tramway leading to this point.	

Army Form C. 2118.

WAR DIARY
107th Coy M.G.C.
or
INTELLIGENCE SUMMARY
(Erase heading not required.)

Instructions regarding War Diaries and Intelligence Summaries are contained in F. S. Regs., Part II. and the Staff Manual respectively. Title Pages will be prepared in manuscript.

Place	Date	Hour	Summary of Events and Information	Remarks and references to Appendices
	6.12.16		Little enemy Machine Gun Fire. 2000 rounds fired on SLOPING ROOF FARM and BIRTHDAY FARM. 1250 rounds on foll. points BONE POINT, IN DE KROISSTRAT + RDS and 4 HUNS FM.	
	7.12.16		All quiet. 1500 rnds on BIRTHDAY FM + SLOPING ROOF FM, 1000 rnds 4 HUNS FM.	
	8.12.16.		Several H.E. fell near N. MIDLAND Avn? 1750 rnds on strong points, 1250 rnds in neighbourhood of BONE PT + 4 HUNS FM.	
	9.12.16.		Quiet night. 1100 rounds on strong points, including HOSPICE.	
	10.12.16		Greater M.G. activity. 1200 rnds at C.C. & S of L'ENFER FM; 750 rnds HELL FM.	
	11.12.16		Enemy M.G. observed at N 36 d 40.63 cutting his own wire. 2250 rnds enemy roads + C.C.	
	12.12.16		SHELL FM. from shelled with H.E. + trench mortars. 1000 rnds traversed MESSINES & L'ENFER. 1000 rnds HELL FM + HOSPICE.	
	13.12.16		5000 rnds fired during night. Following targets engaged:- MESSINES + RDS TO MIDDLE FM MESSINES to 0.32.b. MESSINES WYTSCHAETE RD	
	14.12.16.		Relief day. Enemy roads traversed between MESSINES + WYTSCHAETE 2000 rounds.	
	15.12.16.		Very quiet day + night. 1000 rounds in vicinity of HELL FM.	

Army Form C. 2118.

WAR DIARY
or
INTELLIGENCE SUMMARY
(Erase heading not required.)

107 Coy M.G.C.

Instructions regarding War Diaries and Intelligence Summaries are contained in F. S. Regs., Part II. and the Staff Manual respectively. Title Pages will be prepared in manuscript.

Place	Date	Hour	Summary of Events and Information	Remarks and references to Appendices
	16.12.16.		Enemy M.G. activity between 4.30 + 5.30 p.m. 1000 rounds at enemy strong points.	
	17.12.16.		Less M.G. fire. 2000 rnds on MESSINES sidehill.	
	18.12.16.		1500 rnds fired to area including HELL FM. MIDDLE FM. L'ENFER WOOD, BIRTHDAY FM and MESSINES sidehill.	
	19.12.16.		1200 rnds fired in to same area as yesterday.	
	20.12.16		2000 rnds fired MESSINES-WYTSCHAETE RD + L'ENFER WOOD.	
	21.12.16.		DIAGONAL DUGOUT completed. 2000 rnds fired at enemy strong points.	
	22.12.16.		1500 rnds on track near MORTAR FM. 1250 rnds at SLOPING ROOF FM BIRTHDAY FM. + HOSPICE.	
	23.12.16		Relief of A.S.C. Secn by B + D.	
	24.12.16.		5000 rounds fired at following targets: BIRTHDAY FM C.T. C.T. O. 25.d. Strong point O.25.a. + C.T. O.31.c.	
	25.12.16.		Working party observed though fog officially Northumberland Ra for. dispersed by own machine guns. 1000 rounds at SLOPING ROOF FM C.T. + HOSPICE.	
	26.12.16.		3000 rounds fired at following points SLOPING ROOF FM. + C.T. at O.32.c. HELL FM. + C.T. O.25.d.	
	27.12.16.		3000 rounds fired on BIRTHDAY FM. SLOPING ROOF FM, HOSPICE + L'ENFER WOOD.	

Army Form C. 2118.

WAR DIARY
or
INTELLIGENCE SUMMARY

(Erase heading not required.)

107th Coy M.G. Corps.

Date	Hour	Summary of Events and Information	Remarks and references to Appendices
28.12.16		Enemy shelled heavily between 2.30 + 3.0 and damaged the loophole of the NORTHUMBERLAND ROAD posn. 2000 rounds fired on L'ENFER WOOD and HOSPICE.	
29.12.16		3500 rounds fired on HOSPICE, BIRTHDAY FM, L'ENFER WOOD + WYTSCHAETE RD. Front M.G. posns taken over from 108th M.G.C. 2 in BENSONS COTTAGE 2 in ISNELL FM. Relief of C Section.	
30.12.16		3000 rounds, harassing M. WYTSCHAETE RD. MESSINES SIDEHILL RD + L'ENFER WOOD.	
31.12.16		Posn in NORTHUMBERLAND ROAD again shelled + one casualty caused. No material damage done to emplacement.	

W P Forbes
Capt.

Army Form C. 2118.

Vol 14
107 Coy M.G. Corps

WAR DIARY
or
INTELLIGENCE SUMMARY
(*Erase heading not required.*)

Place	Date	Hour	Summary of Events and Information	Remarks and references to Appendices
	1-1-17		At 5.30 p.m. a heavy artillery duel started on the left. Fort PINKIE fired 2500 rounds on enemy C.T's and R.E. Dump at MESSINES, 1500 rounds fired on enemy front line from SHELL FARM.	
	2-1-17		The night was quiet. During the day enemy trench mortars active. Some shells fell in vicinity of MEDICINE HAT TRAIL & FORT OSBORNE.	
	3-4-17		FORT PINKIE fired 1000 rounds on BIRTHDAY FARM & REDUNK MESSINES. Enemy had some heavy shells on our rear throughout the day. Trench mortars active. FORT PINKIE fired 1000 rounds on SLOPING ROOF FARM.	
	4-1-17		Enemy M.Gs unusually active also trench mortars.	
	5-1-17		The usual shelling took place, our guns being the more active. Fort Pinkie fired 1000 rounds on BIRTHDAY FM. & SLOPING ROOF FM. NORTH MIDLAND fired 1500 rounds on 4 HUNS FM.	

Army Form C. 2118.

WAR DIARY
or
INTELLIGENCE SUMMARY
(Erase heading not required.)

107 Coy M.G. Corps

Instructions regarding "War Diaries and Intelligence Summaries are contained in F. S. Regs., Part II. and the Staff Manual respectively. Title Pages will be prepared in manuscript.

Place	Date	Hour	Summary of Events and Information	Remarks and references to Appendices
	6-1-17		Shelling on both sides both planes all day and a trench mortar engagement in the afternoon. Enemy used many flares during the night	
	7-1-17		At 12-15 p.m. Hostile aircraft engaged one of our aeroplanes and brought it down in flames behind our own lines. 5 guns fired 7000 rounds during the night.	
	8-1-17		Considerable artillery activity during the day. Our anti aircraft guns brought down enemy plane at 1.30 p.m. Our M.G. did no firing. Night was very quiet.	
	9-1-17		Artillery on both sides active during the day. At 9 p.m. our [?] of our guns opened fire on MESSINES & rendered that sector throughout the night. Enemy M.G. were also active.	
	10-1-17		4 Enemy aeroplanes flew low over our lines about 4 p.m. FORT PINKIE fired 1250 rounds on L'ENFER WOOD.	

Army Form C. 2118.

WAR DIARY
or
INTELLIGENCE SUMMARY
(Erase heading not required.)

107 Coy M.G. Corps

Place	Date	Hour	Summary of Events and Information	Remarks and references to Appendices
	11-1-17		During the day no shelling except on the left between 2-30 am & 4 am. During the night a much lighter was observed apparently near the enemy front line. About 10 p.m. a yellow artillery Rocket was sent up by enemy. FORT PINKIE fired 1750 rounds on HOSTICE CROSSROADS. NORTH MIDLAND fired 2500 rounds on 4 HUNS FM. & L'ENFER WOOD.	
	12-1-17		During the day there was little artillery activity. About 7.30 am. an enemy much light was observed on the left. Our trench mortars & artillery started firing on M.G. co-operated. The enemy sent up 3 green rockets which fell at FORT PINKIE, SHELL FARM & NORTH MIDLAND. Our M.G. fired 8000 rounds from 5 guns.	
	13-1-17		The day was quiet. At night FORT PINKIE fired 1000 rounds on HOSTICE CROSSROADS. NORTHMIDLAND fired 2000 rounds on L'ENFER WOOD & MESSINES CROSSROADS by night and 1000 rounds by day. BENSONS COTTAGE fired 1000 rounds on MESSINES during the day.	

Army Form C. 2118.

WAR DIARY
or
INTELLIGENCE SUMMARY
(Erase heading not required.)

107 Coy M.G. Corps

Place	Date	Hour	Summary of Events and Information	Remarks and references to Appendices
	14-1-17		During the day there was a dense mist. At 10 A.m. enemy machine guns fired along our lines. Our M.Gs retaliated. Remainder of the day quiet. About 11 P.m. a number of green, red + purple flares were sent up along our front. FORT PINRIE fired 1250 rounds on the HOSPICE SHELL FARM fired 1250 rounds on MESSINES X Roads. MOB LANE fired 1000 rounds on " " "	
	15-1-17		Day and night quiet — 1 SHELL Fm fired 1250 rds on MESSINES X Rds. FORT PINRIE fired 1250 Rds. on HOSPICE X Rds.	
	16-1-17		Intermittent Trench Mortar and artillery fire on both sides from 11-30 A.M onwards on both sides. Engine hour working in enemy lines opposite C.2. ONE SHELL Fm. fired 1250 Rds. on MESSINES'S Rd. FORT PINRIE fired 1250 Rds on HOSPICE X Rds.	

Army Form C. 2118.

107 Coy M.G. Corps

WAR DIARY
or
INTELLIGENCE SUMMARY
(Erase heading not required.)

Place	Date	Hour	Summary of Events and Information	Remarks and references to Appendices
	17-1-17		at 4.45 p.m. Enemys line was bombarded by artillery and Trench Mortars, their retaliation was weak. Enemy seen working in trenches opposite NORTHUMBERLAND Rd position. Transport and a traction engine heard NORTH of MESSINES at 10 p.m. 5000 Rds fired on MESSINE X Rds. SLOPING Roof Fm. and WYTSCHAETE Ridge	
	18-1-17		Our front line was bombarded with 5.9 and Heavy T.M's about 10.45 a.m. our artillery retaliated effectively, rest of the day very quiet. FORT PINKIE fired 1500 on MESSINES NORTH MIDLAND 1500 Rds on L'ENFER WOOD	
	19-1-17		a whizz-bang got a direct hit on FORT PINKIE doing little damage 2000 Rds fired on L'ENFER WOOD. Enemy Plane flew high about 10.45 p.m.	
	20-1-17		Small artillery & T.M. duels throughout the day, a real hurricane Coy. duelum in our lines about 11.30 A.M. FORT PINKIE & N. MIDLAND fired 2000 rounds on L'ENFER WOOD	

Army Form C. 2118.

WAR DIARY
or
INTELLIGENCE SUMMARY
(Erase heading not required.)

107 Coy M.G. Corps

Instructions regarding War Diaries and Intelligence Summaries are contained in F. S. Regs., Part II. and the Staff Manual respectively. Title Pages will be prepared in manuscript.

Place	Date	Hour	Summary of Events and Information	Remarks and references to Appendices
	21-1-17		Relief took place. N. MIDLAND fired 1000 rds on L'ENFER WOOD FORT PINKIE fired 1000 Rds on L'ENFER WOOD BENSONS COTTAGE fired 1000 Rds on MESSINES.	
	22-1-17		Considerable aeroplane activity. An enemy machine which tried to cross our lines was driven back. Heavy artillery bombardment all day. An Anti- aircraft howitzer was em[placed?] at FORT PINKIE. N. MIDLAND fired 1000 Rds on MESSINES Rd.	
	23-1-17		An artillery duel started about 9 p.m. and lasted about ½ hour N. MIDLAND fired on L'ENFER WOOD + MESSINES X Rds.	
	24-1-17		Artillery active on both sides during morning. IN MIDLAND was shelled with 5.9. No damage was done. About 4.15 h.m. one of our aeroplanes was brought down in enemy lines. Enemy transport was heard moving MESSINES which was fired on by N. MIDLAND + FORT PINKIE.	

Army Form C. 2118.

WAR DIARY
or
INTELLIGENCE SUMMARY
(Erase heading not required.)

107 Coy M.G.C.

Instructions regarding War Diaries and Intelligence Summaries are contained in F.S. Regs., Part II. and the Staff Manual respectively. Title Pages will be prepared in manuscript.

Place	Date	Hour	Summary of Events and Information	Remarks and references to Appendices
	25-1-16		C Sect moved from BROWNLOW Line to billets at FONTAINE HOUCK near METEREN.	
	26-1-16		A.B.&D Sect were relieved in the line by 108 M.G.Coy. they stayed the night at SHANKILL HUTS near NEUVE EGLISE.	
	27-1-16		A.B.&D Sect moved from SHANKILL HUTS to FONTAINE HOUCK.	
	28-1-16		guns were cleaned + inspected. 2.30 p.m. church parade.	
	29-1-16		7.15 A.M. running. 8.30 A.M. A Sect marched to range near NEUVE EGLISE. B.C.D Sects squad + gun drill. 2.30 p.m. games.	
	30-1-16		7.15 A.M. running. 8.30 A.M. B Sect Range. 9 A.M. A.C.D. parade 2.30 p.m. games.	
	31-1-16		7.15 A.M. Running. 8.30 A.M. C Sect Range. 9 A.M. A.B.D. parade. 2 p.m. games.	

NRCook
Capt
107th Coy M.G.C.

WAR DIARY
or
INTELLIGENCE SUMMARY

Army Form C. 2118.

Vol 15
107 Coy M.G.C.

Place	Date	Hour	Summary of Events and Information	Remarks and references to Appendices
In the Field	1.2.17		The company remained in rest billets near METEREN and carried out programme of training each day. 9.30 a.m. The Officers proceeded by bus to KEMMEL HILL and reconnoitred the defences. 7.15 Running parade. 8.30 a.m. A.B.C. Sect. Range 9 a.m. A.B.C. Sects. went to company drill. 11 a.m. gun drill 12-12.30 saluting 2 h.m. football train.	
	2.2.17	7.15 A.m.	Running parade. 9 A.m. arm gun + coy drill 2 h.m. football and pepper chase.	
	3.2.17	7.15 A.m.	Running parade. 9 A.m. The company did a ten mile route march in fighting order.	
	4.2.17		morning church parade. afternoon football.	
	5.2.17	7.15 A.m.	Running parade. 8.30 A Sect Range 9 - 11.30 Drill + Bayonet fighting. 2.15 h.m. football + Boxing.	

WAR DIARY
or
INTELLIGENCE SUMMARY

(Erase heading not required.)

Army Form C. 2118.

107 Coy M.G.C.

Place	Date	Hour	Summary of Events and Information	Remarks and references to Appendices
	6.2.17		7.15 A.M. Running parade. 9-12. Sect. gun r + gun drill. 12.12.30 musketry. 2 p.m. 9 others.	
	7.2.17		Running 7.15 A.M. 9 A.M. Sect. coy + gun drill. 12-12.30 S.H.&gr. 2.30 p.m. Paper chase.	
	8.2.17		7.15 A.M. Running parade. 9 A.M. Sect + am drill. 10 A.M. coy drill 11 A.M. gun drill. 2 p.m. 9 others + Bayig.	
	9.2.17		7.15 Running parade. 9-10 A.M. Sect and am drill. 10-12.30 Tactical exercise. 2.30 p.m. 9 others match v. 107 T.M.B.	
	10.2.17		In morning coy marched to DRANOUTRE for baths. 2.30 p.m. Football	
	11.2.17		Church parade in morning. Afternoon Bayonet fighting team won Brigade competition.	

Army Form C. 2118.

WAR DIARY
or
INTELLIGENCE SUMMARY
(Erase heading not required.)

107 Coy M.G.C

Instructions regarding War Diaries and Intelligence Summaries are contained in F. S. Regs., Part II. and the Staff Manual respectively. Title Pages will be prepared in manuscript.

Place	Date	Hour	Summary of Events and Information	Remarks and references to Appendices
	12.2.17	8.45 A.M.	D sect gone on range, which could not be used owing to the front.	
		9 A.M.	am. Sect + coy drill. 11-12.30 P.M. Tactical exercise	
		2.30 P.M.	9 others + boxing	
	13.2.17	7.15	Running forward. 8.45 A.M. C Sect range. 9-12.30 Drill + Tactical exercise. 2.45 P.M. Football match v. Best by 8 R.I.R. Rif.	
	14.2.17	7.15	Running forward 9 A.M. Sect. arms & Coy Drill in marching order.	
	15.2.17	7.15 A.M.	Running forward 8.45 A.M. B Sect Range 9 A.M - 12.30 P.M. Tactical Exercise.	
	16.2.17		Final Brigade drill competition won by 107 M.S. Coy. Football match v. beat Coy 9 R.I.R.	
	17.2.17		12 guns were mounted at various Dumps near BAILLEUL for anti-aircraft work. The weather was misty + none were seen.	

Army Form C. 2118.

WAR DIARY
or
INTELLIGENCE SUMMARY
(Erase heading not required.)

107 Coy M.G.C

Place	Date	Hour	Summary of Events and Information	Remarks and references to Appendices
	18.2.17		Brigade cross country run won by 107 m.g.Coy. Two men receiving medals	
	19.2.17		9 A.M. Squad & arm drill 10 A.M. mechanism & stoppages 11 A.M. Boot/pulley 12 noon Cleaning guns. Finds Brigade touring.	
	20.2.17		7-15 Running parade 9-12 Drill mechanism + bootpulley	
	21.2.17		7-15 Running parade 9-12 Drill & mechanism	
	22.2.17		Guns withdrawn from anti aircraft position & kept a gun at HAGEDOORNE	
	23.2.17		A & B Sect 2 guns ea Sect & Head quarters moved to KORTHEPT.	
	24.2.17		A & B Sect & 2 gun ea Sect relieved 10 guns of 109 m.g.Coy. in the trenches in the DOUVE Sector. The guns at HAGEEDOORNE were relieved by 109 M.G.Cy. & moved to FONTAINEHOOCK.	
	25.2.17		D Sect & 2 guns ea Sect moved from FONTAINEHOUCK to KORTHEPT. Our guns did not fire & there was nothing to report.	

Army Form C. 2118.

WAR DIARY
or
INTELLIGENCE SUMMARY
(Erase heading not required.)

107 Coy. City. M.G. Corps

Place	Date	Hour	Summary of Events and Information	Remarks and references to Appendices
South of Hill	26.2.17		at 11.30 a.m. 6 5.7" shells fell around Chateau stable intermittent shelling of Hill 63 during afternoon. at 9.30 p.m. large number of lights were seen on night of PLOEGSTEERT WOOD including red and green lights, but practically no artillery was heard. Enemy unusually quiet.	
	27.2.17		At 2.30 A.M. a heavy trench engine was heard behind enemy lines and again at 6 A.M. Position in rear of front line were shelled at 6.30 A.M. Observation rounds fired by gun near CHATEAU on SCHNITZEL F.M. & trench tramway between SCHNITZEL F.M. & BETHLEHEM F.M.	
	28.2.17		Trench mortars fell in front line at 5.30 A.M. Enemy otherwise very quiet.	

N R Stokes
Capt.

Army Form C. 2118.

WAR DIARY
or
INTELLIGENCE SUMMARY
(Erase heading not required.)

107 Coy. M.G.C.

Nov 16

Place	Date	Hour	Summary of Events and Information	Remarks and references to Appendices
In the Field	1.3.17		The Chateau & stables were shelled in morning & the anti aircraft gun was damaged. Enemy shelled rear of HILL 63 all day. Enemy aircraft over the lines in the afternoon too high for M.G. fire. THATCHED COTTAGE gun fired on SCHNITZEL FM.	
	2.3.17		Enemy artillery were active all day our guns retaliated. A + B Sub 5 were relieved by B + D Sub 5.	
	3.3.17		The day was quiet. Our guns did not fire at night.	
	4.3.17		Artillery was quiet all day but aircraft active. Enemy shelled THATCHED COTTAGE on fire at 2.30 h.m. Enemy aircraft were active during night & 2 of our guns fired on enemy E. To	
	5.3.17		Day quiet and nothing to report.	
	6.3.17		Two of our anti aircraft m.g.s fired 500 rounds against low flying enemy plane without any apparent effect. At 7 h.m. 6 of our guns opened fire on MESSINES area & fired 8,000 rounds.	

Army Form C. 2118.

WAR DIARY
or
INTELLIGENCE SUMMARY
(Erase heading not required.)

107 Coy M.G.C.

Place	Date	Hour	Summary of Events and Information	Remarks and references to Appendices
In the field	7/3/17		Our front quiet. On entire bombardment started on our left at 3.30 h.m. and continued till 6 h.m.	Operation Orders attached.
	8/3/17		Day quiet. Slight "frein" was carried out on enemy trenches in conjunction with artillery. Enemy m.g. active during night.	
	9/3/17		During morning enemy artillery fairly active. At 10 a.m. a hostile aeroplane flew over our lines & remained on about 30 minutes. At 9 h.m. heavy shelling was heard on our right but on our front was quiet.	
	10/3/17		The day was quiet & there was nothing to report.	

Army Form C. 2118.

WAR DIARY
or
INTELLIGENCE SUMMARY
(Erase heading not required.)

107 Coy M.G.C

Place	Date	Hour	Summary of Events and Information	Remarks and references to Appendices
In the Field	11.3.19		Our 10 guns in the trench were relieved by the 2nd & 3rd NEW ZEALAND M.G. Coys. on return withdrawing to KORTE PYP Canal.	
	12.3.19		The 12 guns of B.C. & D Sects relieved the 47th M.G. Bn in the trenches in front of LINDEN HOEK. Head Quarters + A. Sect moved from KORTE PYP to TYRONE FARM. The Sects in the trenches came under command of 47th Iny Brigade.	

Army Form C. 2118.

WAR DIARY
or
INTELLIGENCE SUMMARY
(Erase heading not required.)

167 Coy M.G.C.

Instructions regarding War Diaries and Intelligence Summaries are contained in F.S. Regs., Part II. and the Staff Manual respectively. Title Pages will be prepared in manuscript.

Place	Date	Hour	Summary of Events and Information	Remarks and references to Appendices
In the field	13-3-17		The day was quiet, a few shells falling near S.O.S. 3 of our guns fired 3500 rounds on our roads & enemy support lines during the night. Enemy machine guns fired little.	
	14-3-17		Hostile artillery maintained an intermittent fire enough the day. During the night our guns fired 6000 rounds on L'ENFER WOOD & communication trenches in the vicinity. At 10.30 p.m. there was a bombardment on C.17 to which the enemy replied weakly.	
	15-3-17		Artillery and aircraft active all day, an enemy aeroplane crossed our lines morning & afternoon. During the night our guns carried out their usual night firing programme. Railway traffic heard near MESSINES at 7.30 p.m. Artillery less active. Two balloons seen in direction of MESSINES.	
	16-3-17		During the night our guns fired as usual, enemy machine guns very quiet.	
	17-3-17		Hostile aeroplanes observed on our lines nearly all day, their were mostly engaged by our A.A. guns. Hostile artillery active on our right. Our guns were taken in their S.O.S targets and found satisfactory. Enemy guns quiet.	
	18-3-17		The day & night were particularly quiet. A section relieved by section with lorries	

Army Form C. 2118.

WAR DIARY
or
INTELLIGENCE SUMMARY
(Erase heading not required.)

107 Coy MGC

Place	Date	Hour	Summary of Events and Information	Remarks and references to Appendices
In the Field.	18-3-17 (Contd.)		During the night guns were taken on their MGs/Bogels and transported by	
	19-3-17		3 guns withdrawn from the line during the morning. The day was quiet, and the enemy's artillery was inactive except for a few shells directed near S.P.8. A few trench mortars fell near the MINESHAFT position. A red glow was observed behind a MESSINES between 10 pm & 11pm the night also was quiet.	
	20-3-17		Day & night both quiet. S.O.S signals hoisted at 9.0pm, 9.15pm & 9.30pm. During the day a few trench mortars fell near S.P.6 position. The enemy's artillery was active in counter-battery work. During the night our machine guns fired 10,000 rounds trench tramways v PEIPER WOOD.	
	21-3-17		There was no retaliation.	
	22-3-17		Enemy artillery fairly active up to 2.30pm. Otherwise all quiet during the night. Our guns have little but enemy machine guns were more active.	

WAR DIARY or INTELLIGENCE SUMMARY

Army Form C. 2118.

169 Coy M.G.C.

Place	Date	Hour	Summary of Events and Information	Remarks and references to Appendices
In field	23-3-17		During the day CHINNEY FARM was registered on by enemy artillery trench mortars were apparently registering on parts of our line near the front line. The night was quiet.	
	24-3-17		About 3·30 am enemy machine guns became active and at 3·55 am they opened a heavy fire. At 4·0 am the enemy opened an intense bombardment with all pieces of artillery & trench mortars about 4·10 am green lights were seen whereupon the enemy barrage lifted & no S.O.S. signals going up all our machine guns fired on the enemy front, & support lines & communication trenches, about 15,000 rounds were fired. This continued till about 6 a.m. but no raiding party came across. It is not known if the day was quiet. O. & O. Sections relieved #'s 10 and 16 Kms.	
	25-3-17		Enemy artillery active during the morning mo'ly directed against our batteries. Aeroplane active all day. During the night our machine guns were active on dumps. Battalion HdQrs PROLLYERSHEY - WYTSCHAETE Road.	

WAR DIARY or INTELLIGENCE SUMMARY

Army Form C. 2118.

107 **Coy M.G.C.**

Place	Date	Hour	Summary of Events and Information	Remarks and references to Appendices
Lef Julio	27-3-17		The morning was quiet but during the afternoon the enemy artillery became active against SP6, SP7 & KINGSWAY COMMUNICATION TRENCH. This lasted from 3.30pm to 3.45pm. The gun at MINESHAFT was with drawn to FLUFFY. The night was quiet.	
	27-3-17		2 enemy aeroplanes crossed our line about 7am & dropping lights nothing resulted. From this about midday there was an exchange of trench mortars. All was quiet during the night. Steam traffic heard in the vicinity of MESSINES about 10.30 pm.	
	28-3-17	morg aft	Day & night were both quiet.	
	29-3-17		There was a little artillery fire during the day, the night was exceptionally quiet.	
	30-3-17		Little exchange of artillery fire during the day, during the night the enemy machine guns were active during the early part. A & B Sections relieving C & D in the line.	
	31-3-17		The day & night were both quiet. An enemy aeroplane crossed our lines early in the morning.	E. Coy huis Conly 107 M.G.Cy

2449 Wt. W14957/M90 750,000 1/16 J.B.C. & A. Forms/C.2118/12.

WAR DIARY
or
INTELLIGENCE SUMMARY

Army Form C. 2118.

Vol 17
107 Coy M.G.C.

Place	Date	Hour	Summary of Events and Information	Remarks and references to Appendices
In the Field	1-4-17		Both day and night quiet except for desultory shelling	
	2-4-17		The day was again very quiet. The enemy sent up red flares at 4.10 A.M.	
	3-4-17		Enemy sent a few shells over between 5 & 6 p.m. During night – PICADILLY gun fired 1500 rounds on JUMP POINT + KINGSWAY 1200 rounds on N.30.D.70.75	
	4-4-17		Enemy shells various points in our front line abt 6-30pm. Our mg's fire on L'ENFER WOOD, OCCULT AVENUE + BONE POINT.	
	5-4-17		About 9 p.m. enemy replies to our bombardment by shelling KINGSWAY, PICADILLY + S.P.8. During day several enemy planes flew over our lines. Our M.G. fire 3000 rounds on enemy C.T.s + Strong points	
	6-4-17		During the day enemy planes very active over our lines. At night FRENCHMANS FARM fired 2000 rounds on L'ENFER WOOD.	

Army Form C. 2118.

WAR DIARY
or
INTELLIGENCE SUMMARY
(Erase heading not required.)

167 M.G. Coy

Place	Date	Hour	Summary of Events and Information	Remarks and references to Appendices
Trenches SHANBROEK MOLEN Sector	7-4-17		Enemy opened fire on some of our aeroplanes with a new quick firing gun assembling a him hum. KINGSWAY GUN fired 750 rounds on enemy planes without effect - usual night firing took place.	
	8-4-17		Enemy opened more actively than usual shelling various points during day. at night CHIMNEY FM. fired on HOP POINT + trenchmen from on the T rench tramway at 0.31.A. 30.70.	
	9-4-17		A few exploratory shells fell around CHIMNEY FARM at 9.30 p.m. & f.o. of an enemy machine guns opened at me on enemy eTs + tramline. The enemy were using a new and bright during the night.	
	10-4-17		Day quiet as estab for some enemy shrapnel about 1 p.m. Last few nights flares have been seen in sky resembling reflection of fires behind enemy lines.	

WAR DIARY
or
INTELLIGENCE SUMMARY

(Erase heading not required.)

Army Form C. 2118.

107 m.y. Cy

Place	Date	Hour	Summary of Events and Information	Remarks and references to Appendices
In the Trenches	11-4-17		At B Sect: relieved C + D. Enemy activity nil probably owing to bad weather conditions.	
SHANBROEK MOLEN SECTOR	12-4-17		Nothing to report.	
	13-4-17		At 6 A.M. + 7 A.M. m machine gun fired on enemy. During morning enemy shelled TITE Road + trench mortars S.P.6. + SHELL FARM. Our retaliation was heavy. During night – we fired 6000 rounds on enemy supports.	
	14-4-17		5 enemy aircraft fired on our line about 9.30 A.M. 2 in. was shown with M.G.s + a.a. aircraft guns + they were forced to retire though no hits were observed. During night m.g.s fired on OCCULT AVENUE NAPLES ROW + TRENCH Tramway.	
	15-4-17		Enemy fired a chain of flying pigs to our artillery.	

Army Form C. 2118.

WAR DIARY or INTELLIGENCE SUMMARY

(Erase heading not required.)

167 Coy M.G.C

Place	Date	Hour	Summary of Events and Information	Remarks and references to Appendices
9th do Tunnel	17.4.17	about 1.30 A.M.	Enemy appeared to be looking his own wire & sent up an unusual number of white lights. otherwise quiet	
SHANBROEK SECTOR				
	17.4.17	noon	Some heavy shells fell in neighbourhood of DAYLIGHT CORNER about 10.30 p.m. Enemy m.g.n active during night	
	18.4.17		On the 18th April Draft & gun emplts transport & head quarters marched out of TYRONE FARM with the Bgde for training areas around LUMBRES. The Coy were billeted at LE VAL D'ACQUIN which it reached on 18th April. The 11 gun sepn in the line were relieved by the 108 M.g.Coy on 19th April & marched LE VAL D'ACQUIN by train to STOMER on the evening of 20th April.	
	20.4.17		During 3 weeks in the trenches in April there were no casualties in the Coy. and no event of importance occurred	

Army Form C. 2118.

WAR DIARY
or
INTELLIGENCE SUMMARY

(Erase heading not required.)

107 Coy M.G.C.

Place	Date	Hour	Summary of Events and Information	Remarks and references to Appendices
Training AREA LEVAL D'ACQUIN	24-4-17		Company Training each day. 7-7.45 A.m. Running & march 9-12.30 gun drill, firing on range, mechanism & advanced Drill. 2-4 p.m. small tactics exercises & bringing guns into action from limber.	
	25-4-17			
	26-4-17		Marched out at 7.30 A.m. for Batt. field days. The Battn made attack on villages the M.Gs of this company represented the enemy.	
	27-4-17		The Bn. also made a practice attack over plogged trenches & guns were held in reserve & assisted the infantry until covering fire from the rear.	
	28-4-17		The exercise of the day before was repeated.	
	29-4-17		Sunday. no work except church parades.	

Army Form C. 2118.

WAR DIARY
or
INTELLIGENCE SUMMARY

(Erase heading not required.)

Place	Date	Hour	Summary of Events and Information	Remarks and references to Appendices
	30/4/17		Coy marched from LE VAL D'ACQUIN to WIDERNES.	

N.M. Forbes. Capt.
107 M.G. Coy.

WAR DIARY or INTELLIGENCE SUMMARY

Army Form C. 2118.

Vol 18
107 Coy M.G.C.

Place	Date	Hour	Summary of Events and Information	Remarks and references to Appendices
In the Field	1-5-17		The Coy. on it's way back from training area marches from WIZERNES to HAZEBROUK. D Sec- fell out at ARCQUES & proceeded thence by motor lorry to relieve 4 guns of 57 M.G. Coy. guarding dumps at CAISTRE.	
	2-5-17		The Coy less D sect marched from HAZEBROUK to billets outside METEREN.	
	3-5-17		Cleaning guns, kit inspection & unloading limbers	
	4-5-17		2 guns C Sect- relieved 2 guns 108 M.G. Coy. guarding dumps at HAZEBROUKE.	
	5-5-17 to 9-5-17		Coy. remained at METEREN and carried out training programme. Aimy gun drill, mechanism & stoppages also small tactical schemes.	
	10-5-17		D Sect at CAISTRE was relieved by IX Corps Cavalry.	

Army Form C. 2118.

WAR DIARY
or
INTELLIGENCE SUMMARY

(Erase heading not required.)

107 Coy M.G.C.

Instructions regarding War Diaries and Intelligence Summaries are contained in F.S. Regs., Part II. and the Staff Manual respectively. Title Pages will be prepared in manuscript.

Place	Date	Hour	Summary of Events and Information	Remarks and references to Appendices
In the Line	13/5/17		The 107 M.G. Coy relieved the 108 M.G.Cy. in the line in the SHANBROEK Sector. All 16 guns in the line. Coy H.Q. at Bully Beef FARM. Transport & Q.M. Stores at TYRONE FARM.	
	14/5/17		Enemy guns quiet but hi TM's active at times. Our guns doing a good deal of shelling during day. Rations were brought up on pack mules during this tour.	
	15/5/17		During night M.G. fired 7500 rounds on E.T.S. & back areas. On guns active all day. Enemy shelled DAYLIGHT corner between 7 A.M. & 8 A.M.	
	16/5/17		Our M.G. fired 7000 rounds during night on OCEAN SWITCH, JUMP Pt. & L'ENFER WOOD. Enemy more active than usual especially with T.M's & M.Gs.	

Army Form C. 2118.

WAR DIARY
or
INTELLIGENCE SUMMARY
(Erase heading not required.)

107 Coy M.G.C.

Place	Date	Hour	Summary of Events and Information	Remarks and references to Appendices
In the TRENCHES SPANBROEK SECTOR.	17/5/17		Our M.Gs fired 6000 rounds during night. A bombardment took place between 11hr. & midnight. Enemy shelling KINGSWAY, COOKER FM. and FRENCHMANS FM.	
	18/5/17		During night — M.Gs fired 8000 rounds on L'ENFER WOOD, OCCULT TRENCH & tank park. Enemy fired a few shots into Trench-line at TYRONE FM. Pte Johnson, cold shoer, was killed. Trench-mat moved to Doln. camp on CLAPHAM RD. S.S.D. 9.8.	
	19/5/17		M.Gs carried out usual night-firing. Enemy machine & gun active during night at 8.15 p.m. 3 of our planes flew over lines very low and not many observation balloons on view.	
	20/5/17		107 M.G.Coy relieved by 108 M.G.Coy. & moved to rest billets at TYRONE FM. Relief complete 2 p.m.	

WAR DIARY or INTELLIGENCE SUMMARY

Army Form C. 2118.

Place	Date	Hour	Summary of Events and Information	Remarks and references to Appendices
In the line	21/5/17 to 26/5/17		Work in our lines + trench work carried on every morning. During week parties of officers + N.C.O's proceeded to CHEFPENBERG to view the ground. 10 dpm emplacements were constructed behind hedge south of S.P.8. On the 20th 8 O.R. from each Batt. in the Bde were attached to this Coy.	
SHANBROEK SECTOR	27/5/17		107 M.G. Coy went back into line relieving 108 M.G. Coy. Relief complete 2 p.m.	
	28/5/17		Our M.G's fired during night - to targets engaged by artillery by day. Enemy shelled our back area from 9 h.m. until 10.30 h.m.	
	29/5/17		M.G's fired 7500 rounds during night. Our guns shelled enemy lines all day. Enemy replied during night - on back area.	

Army Form C. 2118.

WAR DIARY
or
INTELLIGENCE SUMMARY

(Erase heading not required.)

107 Coy. M.G.C.

Instructions regarding War Diaries and Intelligence Summaries are contained in F. S. Regs., Part II. and the Staff Manual respectively. Title Pages will be prepared in manuscript.

Place	Date	Hour	Summary of Events and Information	Remarks and references to Appendices
In the trenches	30/5/17		Ten guns active as usual & enemy again shelled back areas. During last few days enemy has attempted to reach our dump. There has also been several fires behind his lines.	
ST ANBROEK SECTOR	31/5/17		Our M.G. fired 11750 rounds on artillery targets. Casualties during month. 1 O.R. killed. 1 O.R. wounded. 1 Officer reinforcement reported from base.	

M.P. Forbes.
Capt.

WAR DIARY or INTELLIGENCE SUMMARY

Army Form C. 2118.

Vol 19
107 Coy M.G.C.

Place	Date	Hour	Summary of Events and Information	Remarks and references to Appendices
SPANBROEK SECTOR	1/6/17 to 5/6/17		8 guns in trenches under two officers & 3 nun per gun. Three gun teams in each borough. Fired on targets given by artillery. Teams were relieved every 24 hours. Head quarters & remainder of Coy billeted at TYRONE FARM, from which they visited the Medic of every trench & made their preparation for going in on the top. Transport lines were at CLAPHAM RD 28 S.W. B.S.M. and had to leave their lines nearly every night owing to shelling. Two mules were slightly wounded. On the 6th Lieut-Walker, Sgt Green & Cpl Moon were killed by shell fire in the trenches. 2-6-17. Lieut J.S. CRESSALL reported to the Coy. Command of the Coy.	
	6/6/17	2 a.m	The 8 guns out of the line + all gun teams moved out into trenches. 10 guns being in A line. N 27.c.8.4. + 6 guns in Reserve line.	
			16 men were attached to Coy from Infantry as carriers	

Army Form C. 2118.

WAR DIARY
or
INTELLIGENCE SUMMARY

(Erase heading not required.)

107 Coy M.G.C.

Instructions regarding War Diaries and Intelligence Summaries are contained in F.S. Regs., Part II. and the Staff Manual respectively. Title Pages will be prepared in manuscript.

Place	Date	Hour	Summary of Events and Information	Remarks and references to Appendices
SPANDBROEK SECTOR	7/6/17	3/10 A.M.	The Coy took part in the advance of 2nd Army. Account of Operation attached.	
	8/6/17		at 4 A.M. The Coy were withdrawn to BEEHIVE DUGOUTS. & cela- 4 guns in reserve positions	
On the field	9/6/17	11A.M.	Coy moved to rest camp at S.II.A. The 4 guns in reserve positions being withdrawn & marching off at 2 P.M.	
	10/6/17		Church parade. Moved in afternoon to camp beside transport at S.S.D.	
	11/6/17		Inspection of Kit & Box respirators by Lt Offeers. Inspection field marching order by O.C. Company	
	12/6/17		Gun Drill mechanism & stoppages.	

Army Form C. 2118.

WAR DIARY
or
INTELLIGENCE SUMMARY
(Erase heading not required.)

107 Coy M.G.C.

Instructions regarding War Diaries and Intelligence Summaries are contained in F. S. Regs., Part II. and the Staff Manual respectively. Title Pages will be prepared in manuscript.

Place	Date	Hour	Summary of Events and Information	Remarks and references to Appendices
In the Field	13/6/17	2.30 p.m.	Company marched into new camp at LA BOURSE Nr BAILLEUL.	
	14/6/17	7 a.m. 9 a.m.	Running Parade. Cleaning Limbers and Lecture on Map reading	
	15/6/17		Parade gun drill mechanism & stoppages Capt Forbes left by for Home Establishment. Capt. J.S. Conrad took over command.	
	16/6/17	6.30 a.m. 9am to 11.30	Physical training Limber Parades and Lectures	
	17/6/17	10 am	Church Parade.	
	18/6/17		Company move but towards the line coming for the night - near start 7 m	

A.F.

Army Form C. 2118.

WAR DIARY
or
INTELLIGENCE SUMMARY
(Erase heading not required.)

107 Coy M.G.C.

Place	Date	Hour	Summary of Events and Information	Remarks and references to Appendices
	19/6/19	2 p.m.	Coy by motor lorries from Steenvoorde to camp at BULLY BEEF.	
		9.30 p.m.	No 4 Sect took over 4 guns in the line from 32 M.G. Coy. No 1 & No 3 Sects relieved 8 guns of 34 M.G. Coy. These guns were situated on East side of MESSINES WSCHAETE RD in the neighbourhood of guns RD. No 2 Sect remained in reserve at Coy H.Q. Relief completed 2.30 A.M.	
	20/6/19		Position consolidated – quiet – any guns did not fire.	
	21/6/19		Desultory shelling from enemy throughout day. Enemy planes seen over our lines flying low at 5.30 A.M. & 6 P.M.	
	22/6/19		Operations NIL. Usual shelling by enemy.	
	23/6/19		Artillery activity normal. A new band was observed approaching from enemy lines.	

Army Form C. 2118.

WAR DIARY
or
INTELLIGENCE SUMMARY
(Erase heading not required.)

103 Coy M.G.C.

Place	Date	Hour	Summary of Events and Information	Remarks and references to Appendices
	24/6/17		No 2 Sect relieved No 4 Sect in the night. 4th Sect No 4 going into Reserve at BULLY BEEF F.M.	
	25/6/17		Situation Normal. Usual shelling.	
	26/6/17		Usual shelling, about 10 shells fell near our left 1" gun. One or 2 rounds for anti-air. drove off an enemy aeroplane which attached our Observation balloon.	
	27/6/17		The Company was relieved by 111th M.G.Coy. Relief complete 2.45 A.M. On completion of relief sect of transport marched to TYRONE F.M. Casualties during tour in trenches NIL.	
	28/6/17		Cleaning up & flushing C. in hrs.	

Army Form C. 2118.

WAR DIARY
or
INTELLIGENCE SUMMARY
(Erase heading not required.)

Place	Date	Hour	Summary of Events and Information	Remarks and references to Appendices
	29/4/17	8 A.M.	Company Marched from TYRONE FM to OULTERSTEENE nr BAILLEUL.	
	30/6/17.		Parades 9 A.M to 12 Noon. Sects at defence of Sect commanders. Casualties during Month. 1 Officer 3 O.R. killed 6 O.R wounded.	S. Coyne Lieut pr o.c. 107 m.t.b.

Army Form C. 2118.

WAR DIARY
or
INTELLIGENCE SUMMARY

(Erase heading not required.)

Vol 20

107 Coy M.G.C.

Instructions regarding War Diaries and Intelligence Summaries are contained in F. S. Regs., Part II. and the Staff Manual respectively. Title Pages will be prepared in manuscript.

Place	Date	Hour	Summary of Events and Information	Remarks and references to Appendices
In the Field	1-7-17 to		The Coy remained in rest at OUTTERSTEENE carrying on usual Sect Offrin	
	4-7-17		The Coy moved from OUTTERSTEENE to CAESTRE marching off at 7 A.M.	
	5-7-17		The Coy marched from CAESTRE to RENNESCURE marched off 5.40 A.M.	
	6-7-17		The Coy marched from RENNESCURE to LE VAL D'ACQUIN marched off 4 A.M.	
	8-7-17		Church parade in morning afternoon Sect Offrin parades.	
	9-7-17		6.30 – 7.15 Physical training 8.30 C.O's inspection 9 – 12.45 parades under Sect Offrin afternoon games.	
	10-7-17		Parade as for 9th ault.	

WAR DIARY or INTELLIGENCE SUMMARY

Army Form C. 2118.

107 Coy M.G.C.

Place	Date	Hour	Summary of Events and Information	Remarks and references to Appendices
In the field	1-7-17 to 4-7-17		The Coy remained in rest at OUTTERSTEENE. Training, carried on until last officers	
	5-7-17		The Coy moved from OUTTERSTEENE to CAESTRE arriving off 7AM	
	6-7-17		The Coy moved from CAESTRE to RENNESCURE arrived off 5.40 AM	
	7-7-17		The Coy moved from RENNESCURE to LE VAL D'ACQUIN arriving off 4 AM	
	8-7-17		Cleaned kit. & making strava huts. Officers hunted.	
	9-7-17		6.30–9.15 Physical training 9.30 "G" actions 1–11.45 Parade under Sub Officers.	
	10-7-17		Parade as for 9th inst.	

Army Form C. 2118.

WAR DIARY
or
INTELLIGENCE SUMMARY
(Erase heading not required.)

107th M.G. Co.

Place	Date	Hour	Summary of Events and Information	Remarks and references to Appendices
In the Field	11th		Physical Training. C.O's Inspection. Range Practice.	
	12th		Company Sports Meeting.	
	13th			
	15th		Brigade training at Tilques AREA.	
	20th			
	22nd		Company moved to billets at SETQUES	
	23rd			
	24th		Bde training at SETQUES. TILQUES AREA.	
	24th		Moved to billets WINNIZELE AREA.	
	25th		Section under Section Officer	
	26th		Section under Section Officer	
	27th		Sections under Section Officer	
	28th		Section under Section Officer. Weather fine, very warm.	
	29th		morning wet	
	30th		Section under Section Officer. Wet morning. Company moved to Watou area.	
	31st		Billets near WATOU West Vlg	

Army Form C. 2118.

WAR DIARY
or
INTELLIGENCE SUMMARY

(Erase heading not required.)

10TH M G Co

Place	Date	Hour	Summary of Events and Information	Remarks and references to Appendices
In the field	11th		Physical training. C.O's Inspection. Range Duel.	
	12th		Company Sports meeting.	
	13th		Then	
	20th		Brigade training at the Tilques. AREA	
	20th		Company moved to Lieuts of Setques	
	21st		Bn training at Setques. Tilques AREA	
	24th		Moved to Lieuts Winnizele AREA	
	25th		Section under Section officer	
	26th			
	27th		Sections under Section Officers weather fine, very warm	
	28th		turning wet	
	30th		Section under Section Officers. We mummy company moved to Watou	
	31st		area. WATOU wet day	

WAR DIARY *or* **INTELLIGENCE SUMMARY**
(Erase heading not required.)

Army Form C. 2118.

Vol 21

10TH M.G. Co.

Place	Date	Hour	Summary of Events and Information	Remarks and references to Appendices
In the field	1-8-17	m	Wet day.	
	2-8-17	pm	Company moved up East of YPRES and took over newly captured ground from 164th, 165th, 166th, 195th M.G. Cos of 55th Div. Wet day, ground in awful condition. Casualties Pte THOMPSON killed, Pte HAYES wounded, Pte EVANS missing, the gun destroyed by shell.	
	3-8-17	pm	Very wet day. Casualties Pte LEADBETTER wounded.	
	4-8-17		Bright day. Artillery on both sides more active. Enemy sniping rapidly. S.O.S. went up three times. One barrage gun fired 10,000 rounds, terrific firing position in shell holes. Pte LOVELESS wounded. Special pod of R.I.R.	
	5-8-17		S.O.S. went up from our lines. Barrage guns fired 20,000 rounds. Enemy went by all ranks especially LIEUT. A. DENT-YOUNG, and LIEUT. ALLKINS. Also Ptes LINDSAY and APPLEYARD. Casualties killed L.Cp OWEN & Pte PRICE. Wounded CPL MILLER Pte LOGIE, L.Cp KENDLTY, L.Cp GAULT, Pte WALSH, Pte MYLES, Pte GETTY. O.R. from 8.R.I.R.	

WAR DIARY or INTELLIGENCE SUMMARY

Army Form C. 2118.

107th M.G.Co.

Place	Date	Hour	Summary of Events and Information	Remarks and references to Appendices
In the field	6.8.17		S.O.S. sent up from line. Enemy trying to exit our trenches, but stopped by artillery & M.G. barrage. Our M.guns fired 50,000 rounds in 35 minutes. Situation became quieter. Difficulty in getting up ammunition owing to saturated state of ground.	
	7.8.17		Eight guns relieved in line by four guns of 108th M.G.Co. & four guns of 109th M.G.Co. Men completely exhausted from exposure.	
	8.8.17		Eight gun crews from the line. Situation normal. Killed Pt PARKER. Wounded L-Cp WILSON, Pt McCLURE, Cpl TURTINGTON, Pt HOUSTON.	
	9.8.17		Gun destroyed by fire in BLACK LINE (front line). Situation normal. Killing Pt SEYMOUR, Pt SMITH. Wounded CPL HILL.	
	10.8.17		Situation normal. Working party taking ammunition to BLACK LINE caught in barrage. Killed L-Cp SCOTT. Wounded Pt CARTLEDGE, Pt SPEAR, Pt WILSHER.	
	11.8.17		Situation normal. Enemy stonked at ??? Bennetts company hard hit. ??? sufficiently in enemy S.F.A. bore down ???(?) ??? ??? patrols in BLUE LINE without success.	

Army Form C. 2118.

WAR DIARY
or
INTELLIGENCE SUMMARY

(Erase heading not required.)

107th M.G.C.

Place	Date	Hour	Summary of Events and Information	Remarks and references to Appendices
In the field.	12.8.17		Situation normal, weather showery. O.C. 107th M.G.C. assumed command of all thrusting guns in the line, relieving O.C. 109th M.G.Co. in MELITTE DUG OUTS.	
	13.8.17		Day very quiet. Section in Right Sector of Black line suffering from Bad feet due to water logged trenches.	
	14.8.17 to 16.8.17		See attached. Lt F. MILLS and 38 O.R. join company.	
	19.8.17 to 22.8.17		Company entrained at VLAMERTINGE for WINNEZELE area.	
	23.8.17		C. organising Company. Drafts of in Officer, 2Lt HISCOCK + 22 O.R. arrived	
	24.8.17		Company entrained at ESQUELBECK for BAPAUME. M.G. training	

Army Form C. 2118.

WAR DIARY
or
INTELLIGENCE SUMMARY

(Erase heading not required.)

107TH M.G.C.

Place	Date	Hour	Summary of Events and Information	Remarks and references to Appendices
In the field	25.8.17	—	M.G. training. Four Officers & 4 O.R. proceed to reconnoitre the TRESCAULT Area, presently held by SOUTH AFRICAN M.G.C. 9th DIV.	
	26.8.17	—	M.G. training	
	27.8.17	—	Company moved to YTRES area.	
	28.8.17	—	M.G. training. Weather stormy & windy.	
	29.8.17	—	Company relieved SOUTH AFRICAN M.G.C. & 4 guns of 19TH M.G.C. in owing onwards	
	30.8.17	—	Quiet day, little shelling, heavy bottled M.G. fire on left, flare on turn.	
	31.8.17	—	Quiet day, no M.G. activity	

Confidential   104th. Coy.
                                            M. G. Corps.
<u>104th. Infantry Brigade.</u>

Report on Operations of the above Company
           on the 16th. August, 1917.

The Company was detailed to fire a Barrage in front of the Advancing Troops.

Positions were chosen in the BLACK LINE and the Company divided into two Batteries of 8 Guns each, called "Y" and "Z" Batteries respectively.

"Y" Battery was placed in CARRICORN TRENCH and was under the command of LT. L.G. BOLTON. assisted by LT. J. BARKER and 2/LT. J.P. BUDGEN.

"Z" Battery was placed in DUST TRENCH, "POMMERN", and was under the command of LT. A.W. ALLKINS. assisted by LT. A.J. DENT-YOUNG and 2/LT. K.J.N. HANSELL.

Eight Guns having been employed in the Defence of the Sector, from the day the Division took over the Command, in the BLACK LINE, it only remained to get 8 Guns up to their Positions, this was done 4 hours before Zero, without any difficulty or casualties.

Company Head Quarters was established near POMMERN in DUST TRENCH at Zero — 5 hours, and the Operations were controlled from there.

By Zero, all Guns, Ammunition and Water, were in position, ready to open fire at Zero + 30 as per Schedule attached.

107th. Coy.,
M.G. Corps.

Confidential.
107th. Infantry Brigade

At Zero -10 All Guns were mounted & laid ready to fire and the Company "Stood To."

Zero. Our Artillery Barrage opened. The Infantry immediately went forward following close behind the Barrage, and were followed by successive waves. The first wave was through the enemy's BARRAGE, before he opened fire. The second wave appeared to only have a few casualties, and by the time the third wave arrived, there was no Barrage, and the enemy's artillery was firing very wild, shells dropping all over the place.

The Infantry appeared to meet with no opposition, this side of HILL 35 and did not seem to have taken many casualties.

Zero + 30. Our Guns opened fire & kept up a rate of 1 Belt per Gun every 5 minutes, all Guns working & firing splendidly. This was continued until Zero + 40.

Zero + 40. The Barrage was lifted 100 yards every 5 minutes until :-

Zero + 85. when Infantry were observed coming back over the crest of HILL 35. I immediately sent out to find out what was happening, and all my observer could see, was that the Infantry were retiring, and he could see no enemy. Unfortunately, this observer was killed, later in the day.

Confidential   107th. Coy.
                                             16. G. Corps.

107th. Infantry Brigade.

This flanked the fire of the Guns for a few minutes.

At Zero +110. I received a message from LIEUT. L.G. BOLTON, O.C. "Y" Battery, timed 6.25 a.m. saying Infantry were coming back. On going over, I found this to be so.

At Zero +160. Infantry came back to the BLACK LINE. About an hour and a half after this, a concentrated bombardment was opened on the BLACK LINE. I had 3 Guns knocked out, and several casualties.

SUPPLIES. Thanks to the assistance lent to the Company by the 107th. Infantry Brigade we were able to get more ammunition than was required, up before Zero. Also this gave the Company an opportunity of getting water up.

At Zero. LT. J.H. ROBSON led 16 Pack Animals up to the BLACK LINE from WIELTJE and brought up fresh supplies of ammunition and water for the Guns.

This was an exceedingly good & daring performance.

Confidential.   104th. Coy.
                                                 M. G. Corps.
104th. Infantry Brigade.

The Guns fired over 130,000 Rounds in all, and worked splendidly. Great difficulty was experienced in keeping Belts dry, but this was soon rectified with the fresh supply arriving with the Pack Transport. All ranks behaved splendidly.

Casualties during Operations.

Killed.

    No. 27022, L/Cpl. Dunn, C. H.
    "   94659, Pte.   Hand, G. H.
    "   24808, "   Kennedy, J.

Wounded.

    No. 30994, L/Cpl. Watts, C. J.
    "   8243. Pte.   Livins, B.
    "   8268. Cpl.   Lark, A.
    "   31494. Pte.   Dickerson, J. E.
    "   24823. "   Bell, W. T.
    "   24811   "   Swain, S.
    "   14551   "   Cox, A.
    Lieut. A. J. Dent-Young.

Missing.

    No. 8264, Pte. McGrath, J.

16/8/17

J. Cussell Capt.
O.C. 104 Coy
M.G.C

Army Form C. 2118.

YA 22

WAR DIARY
or
INTELLIGENCE SUMMARY

(Erase heading not required.)

Instructions regarding War Diaries and Intelligence Summaries are contained in F. S. Regs., Part II. and the Staff Manual respectively. Title Pages will be prepared in manuscript.

107 Co M.G.C.

Place	Date	Hour	Summary of Events and Information	Remarks and references to Appendices
In the field	1·9·17	A.M.	4000 rounds fired during the night on TRIANGLE WOOD, H 34 a at suspected working parties, & at the GLADE. Enemy very quiet, little hostile M.G. activity. COSY COPSE shelled at intervals.	
	2·9·17	p.m.	Enemy shelled BILHAM + DERBY RESERVE. 3000 rounds fired on HAVRINCOURT VILLAGE & a white tape put out by enemy to mark a new trench. Two hostile aeroplanes came over our lines during the night.	
	3·9·17	a.m.	Very quiet day. 1000 rounds fired on dumps K 28 b 40–20, TRIANGLE WOOD & Sunken road K 36 b. Enemy plane passed over our lines during the night.	
	4·9·17	p.m.	2250 t.b. fired on Road K 36 c 00 – 15 to 70 – 70, & HAVRINCOURT VILLAGE. Enemy very quiet. Weather very bright.	
	5·9·17		More aerial activity, enemy from atmy crossing our lines at intervals. Enemy plane dropped six bombs at 10·30 P.M. near H 36 c + TRIANGLE WOOD. 1000 rounds fired on H 36 c + TRIANGLE WOOD	

Army Form C. 2118.

WAR DIARY
or
INTELLIGENCE SUMMARY

(Erase heading not required.)

Instructions regarding War Diaries and Intelligence Summaries are contained in F. S. Regs., Part II. and the Staff Manual respectively. Title Pages will be prepared in manuscript.

107th Co M.G.C

Place	Date	Hour	Summary of Events and Information	Remarks and references to Appendices
In the Field.	6.9.17	pm.	Uneventful day. Enemy Aeroplanes active but kept at a great height during the day.	
	7.9.17	pm.	Enemy artillery more active. Aerial activity not so marked.	
	8.9.17	pm.	8500 rounds fired during night on enemy line of communication & places where movement had been observed.	
	9.9.17	pm.	Uneventful day. Some enemy T.M. activity on our reserve line (DERBY RESERVE). Bright warm day.	
	10.9.17	pm.	Hostile artillery much more active. Bright day after misty morning.	
	11.9.17	pm.	Hostile artillery less active. M.G.s fired on enemy working parties & every known line of communication & on thin on our line in the evening.	

Army Form C. 2118.

WAR DIARY
or
INTELLIGENCE SUMMARY.
(Erase heading not required.)

10th C. M.G.C.

Instructions regarding War Diaries and Intelligence Summaries are contained in F. S. Regs., Part II. and the Staff Manual respectively. Title pages will be prepared in manuscript.

Place	Date	Hour	Summary of Events and Information	Remarks and references to Appendices
The Field	12.9.17	PM.	M.Gs fired 5000 rounds on X roads behind enemy lines + 250 rds into HAVRINCOURT.	
			Low aerial activity. Quiet day. Weather bright + dry.	
"	13.9.17	PM	M.Gs fired 8000 rounds on outskirts of HAVRINCOURT. Saw enemy artillery activity on back areas.	
	14.9.17		M.Gs fired 8000 rounds on outskirts of HAVRINCOURT commencing at 11:31 P.M. in conjunction with a gas projector attack against that place.	
			Explosion seen behind enemy lines.	
	15.9.17		M.Gs fired 1000 rounds during the night on enemy trenches. Enemy aeroplanes were active flying low over our lines, engaged by our AA Machine guns.	
	16.9.17		In conjunction with artillery on M.Guns fired 4500 rounds on enemy's back areas.	
			Enemy retaliated on TRESCAULT + METZ-TRESCAULT RD.	
	17.9.17		M.G's fired 9000 rounds in conjunction with artillery on enemy's back areas during the night. Enemy M.G. were quite keen used in was enemy artillery.	
			Light Signals were observed behind enemy's lines, several red + white.	
	18.9.17		A barrage programme was carried out with artillery our M.guns firing 7000 rounds on back areas, 1500 rounds were fired in conjunction with	

WAR DIARY
or
INTELLIGENCE SUMMARY.
(Erase heading not required.)

Army Form C. 2118.

Instructions regarding War Diaries and Intelligence Summaries are contained in F. S. Regs., Part II. and the Staff Manual respectively. Title pages will be prepared in manuscript.

Place	Date	Hour	Summary of Events and Information	Remarks and references to Appendices
Field	18-9-17		Trench Mortar Battery on enemy OPs fired 80 T.O. Enemy artillery shelled roads	
			and back areas.	
	19-9-17		METZ-GOUZEAUCOURT in WINCHESTER VALLEY with heavy shells. Two in guns quiet. Our M guns fired 5,500 rounds in conjunction with defence scheme brought into operation. Enemy artillery on enemy trench system + back areas. Enemy M guns were remarkably quiet. his artillery was however rather more active. Enemy aeroplane crossed our lines + was engaged by our A.A. M. Gun.	
	20-9-17		5,000 rounds fired during the night in conjunction with artillery programme. 250 rounds against Gonnelieu. Enemy artillery was active against Gouzeaucourt Wood otherwise quiet. Enemy aeroplane	
	21-9-17		6,000 rounds fired in conjunction with artillery. Quiet day + night	
	22-9-17		During the day the enemy artillery was active but during the night it was quiet. his machine guns however showed the greater activity than usual During a raid by the brigade on right there was little reply from Our guns fired 6,500 in conjunction with artillery	
	23-9-17		4,000 rounds fire during the night. Enemy artillery were our gun at BUISSON We also shelled METZ doing little damage.	

Army Form C. 2118.

WAR DIARY
or
INTELLIGENCE SUMMARY.
(Erase heading not required.)

Instructions regarding War Diaries and Intelligence Summaries are contained in F. S. Regs., Part II. and the Staff Manual respectively. Title pages will be prepared in manuscript.

Place	Date	Hour	Summary of Events and Information	Remarks and references to Appendices
Irfoy	24-9-17		Artillery being suspected we co-operated with our artillery by bringing harassing fire to on his back areas. 5300 rounds were expended. Enemy M guns very active against our aeroplanes.	
	25-9-17		Situation normal & quiet.	
	26-9-17		During the day artillery was active on various fronts several shells falling near our gun at BILHEM. Aircraft inactive. Unusual quiet time of	
	27-9-17		Our guns fired 6500 on targets in conjunction with the artillery. A conference took place between a representative of this company the Brigadier General, Artillery, & Divis Guns officers & J.M.B. a concerted programme of harassing fire was stuff devised to come into operation on — after 1h. 28th inst.	
	28-9-17		Our M/gs fired 2000 as per programme arranged with artillery. Activity normal.	
	29-9-17		Our artillery supplied some harassed in HARINCOURT, shorts & galloping horses were heard after a salvo. Enemy artillery normal. Our M/guns fired 8000 rds.	
	30-9-17		Enemy artillery shelled our balloon without success. Our guns normally active. Several Enemy planes crossed line	

WAR DIARY / INTELLIGENCE SUMMARY

Army Form C. 2118.

137H MGC

Place	Date	Hour	Summary of Events and Information	Remarks and references to Appendices
Field	1/10/17		Day normal, during night our guns fired 6000 rounds on enemy lines of communication & 2 belts on an enemy gun.	
	2/10/17		Harassing fire was continued throughout the night. 5000 rounds being fired. The period was normal.	
	3/10/17		Enemy artillery active on our light railways otherwise quiet on our refused flank. Fired 4000 rounds on both areas.	
	4/10/17		Our machine guns fired 4000 rounds in conjunction with artillery. Period normal.	
	5/10/17		Gas was projected into HAVRINCOURT during which our m.gs fired 1500 rounds. Was also fired to during the night. Brigade on right did a successful raid. C.O. returned from leave.	
	6/10/17		4000 rounds fired in conjunction with artillery. Period normal.	
	7/10/17		Enemy tried a raid but failed to capture any prisoners. Our fire 4000 rounds on usual target otherwise normal.	
	8/10/17		Enemy attempted another raid on "B" sap, he failed to take any prisoners but left one dead officer and 1 slightly wounded man. Our guns fired as usual.	

Army Form C. 2118.

WAR DIARY
or
INTELLIGENCE SUMMARY.
(Erase heading not required.)

107TH M.G.C.

Place	Date	Hour	Summary of Events and Information	Remarks and references to Appendices
In the Field	9/10/17		The raiders on enemy's line our took one prisoner killing four, the remainder of the post. Our guns fired an enormous number of rounds in view of probable enemy relief being expected. Lieut Wilson went on leave.	
	10/10		Period normal. 4800 rounds fired at night.	
	11/10		Period Quiet, our guns firing 20 rounds	
	12/10		Less activity than usual. We fired 4800 rounds to our front	
	13/10		Normal activity more movement than usual, an enterprise by the 1st R.I.F. did not prove successful.	
	14/10		Rather more activity Harassing Linial lights observed with the usual. Harassing fire carried on.	
	15/10		Normal activity 4800 rounds fired as normal	
	16/10		In co-operation with the artillery we fired 4000 rounds harassing fire	
	17/10		More activity, we fired on usual artillery targets	
	18/10		Rather more activity than usual, enemy shelling BLIGHTY +BASS Lents, our guns firing on BOGGARTS HOLE when work was in progress.	

D. D. & L., London, E.C.
(A.283) Wt. W.8697/M.1672 50,000 4/17 Sch 52a Forms/C/2118/14

WAR DIARY
or
INTELLIGENCE SUMMARY.
(Erase heading not required.)

Army Form C. 2118.

191st M.G.C.

Place	Date	Hour	Summary of Events and Information	Remarks and references to Appendices
	19/10		Normal night firing, otherwise rather increased activity. hu fire	
			4000 according to programme. a 1500 m special target.	
	20.10		BILHEM war gun section also BATTN HQ. on fire on	
			usual programme, also 1500 m special target (enemy wiring in	
			K3UC 0030.	
	21.10		Enemy Artillery fairly active. HAVRINCOURT WOOD.	
			BILHEM, ALFRED ROAD and COSY COPSE received	
			attention. With our own fire in selected targets by	
			night in conjunction with artillery.	
	22.10		Enemy Artillery less active. some T.M. activity in retaliation	
			to our own. Our fired by M.G. on selected targets	
			throughout the night in conjunction with artillery.	
	23.10		Hostile Artillery fairly active. Our own fire in conjunction	
			with artillery harassing fire.	
	24.10		Enemy Artillery normal. Novel M.G. nights from	
			harassed round, our own, with artillery.	

WAR DIARY or INTELLIGENCE SUMMARY

Army Form C. 2118.

107th M G Co

Place	Date	Hour	Summary of Events and Information	Remarks and references to Appendices
Field	24.10	A.M.	1000 rounds fired by day on selected targets	
"	25.10		Enemy Artillery active on our front line. 3000 rounds fired on enemy movement according to programme by night. 200 rds on enemy movement by day.	
"	26.10	P.M.	Track to BILHEM shelled with gas shells + HE at 9.P.M. 3000 rds fired per programme. Some enemy M.G. activity	
"	27.10	A.M.	about 10 a.m. Enemy T.M's fired on BOAR COPSE. 3000 rounds fired by M.G. according to programme	
"	28.10	A.M.	Enemy AA machine guns active throughout the day. Enemy active on his usual Targets. 3000 rds fired during the night as usual	
"	29.10	A.M.	Hostile aeroplanes flew over our line at 5.P.M. Day very quiet TRESCAULT shelled at 9 A.M. 3000 rds fired as usual during the night. 1000 by day in conjunction with Artillery	
"	30.10	A.M.	some T.M. activity on hostile sides. 2000 rds fired on enemy movement during the day. 1000 rds according to programme during the night.	

WAR DIARY
or
INTELLIGENCE SUMMARY.

107 H G Coy

Army Form C. 2118.

Place	Date	Hour	Summary of Events and Information	Remarks and references to Appendices
Field	31.10	PM	Enemy activity normal. Aeroplane seen descending in flames thulind enemy lines at 4.15 P.T. trees recently planted by enemy to conceal programme.	

Army Form C. 2118.

107 M.G. Coy

WAR DIARY
or
INTELLIGENCE SUMMARY.
(Erase heading not required.)

Instructions regarding War Diaries and Intelligence Summaries are contained in F. S. Regs., Part II, and the Staff Manual respectively. Title pages will be prepared in manuscript.

Hour, Date, Place			Summary of Events and Information	Remarks and references to Appendices
In the Field	1	XI-17	3000 rounds fired as per programme. Hostile artillery active COSY COPSE & TRESCAULT receiving attention.	
"	2	XI-17	Increased hostile artillery activity. Attempts made on "B" sap. 4000 rounds fired to programme.	
"	3	XI-17	3000 rds fired to programme at 8.45 pm hostile art. bombarded the front line trenches.	
"	4	XI-17	3000 rds fired per programme 2000 on taps in wire. BILHEM received attention from hostile artillery. 2 Lt R.F. MERCHANT joined the Coy.	
"	5	XI-17	4000 rds to programme 3000 on taps in wire. Hostile artillery quiet. BILHEM received attention.	
"	6	XI-17	Hostile artillery practically inactive. 4000 rds to programme & 3500 on taps in wire. 2 Lt G.H. PUGH & 32 O.R. joined from Bapaume.	
"	7	XI-17	Hostile artillery active all along Front line system. 4000 rds to programme 2800 on taps in wire. CPL LARK rejoined coy.	
"	8	XI-17	Hostile artillery less active. COSY COPSE & TRESCAULT received attention. 4000 rds to programme 3000 on taps in wire.	
"	9	XI-17	Artillery quiet. 4000 rds to programme 2750 on taps in wire.	
"	10	XI-17	Hostile Artillery practically inactive. 4000 to programme & 3000 on taps in wire.	
"	11	XI-17	4000 rds to programme & 2500 on taps in wire. Artillery inactive owing to Fog.	

WAR DIARY
or
INTELLIGENCE SUMMARY.
(Erase heading not required.)

Army Form C. 2118.

M25 107th Co MGC

Instructions regarding War Diaries and Intelligence Summaries are contained in F. S. Regs., Part II., and the Staff Manual respectively. Title pages will be prepared in manuscript.

Hour, Date, Place			Summary of Events and Information	Remarks and references to Appendices
In the field	1	XII	17 1/B Coy left COURCELLES - LE - COMPTE & proceeded to BEAULENCOURT	
"	2	XII	" 1/B Coy proceeded to LECHELLE	
"	3	XII	" 1/B Guns & equipment cleaned & sections reorganised	
"	4	XII	" 1/B In view of taking over part of the line	
"	5	XII	" 1/B Coy proceeded to S E corner of HAVRINCOURT WD	
"	6	XII	" 1/B Nos 3 & 4 sections took over part of the line from 98th M G Coy	
"			" 1/B Nos 1 & 2 sections took up commanding positions on HIGHLAND RIDGE.	
"	7	XII	" 1/B Coy HQs moved into HIGHLAND RIDGE & 108th Coy took command of 16 guns of 107 Coy.	
"	8	XII	" 1/B Hostile artillery very active throughout the day & night. Chiefly on back area.	
"	9	XII	" 1/B Hostile artillery M Gs quieter. Heavy Frost at night. In consequence 1000 rounds fired on enemy approaches to Keep from known. CPL MURPHY wounded	
"	10	XII	" 1/B Low visibility. Hostile activity quieter. 9 EAs came over. Bombed 116 back area	
"	11	XII	" 1/B Enemy fairly quiet. Pte WARD, H.A. self inflicted wound	
"	12	XII	" 1/B Enemy fairly quiet. Numerous shelling of back area by hostile artillery. Several EAs here patrolling	

(108.) Wt. 3699.—851. 50,000. 10/1914.—A. T. & Co., Ltd. Forms/C. 2118/10.

WAR DIARY or INTELLIGENCE SUMMARY

Army Form C. 2118.

107th M.G.C

Place	Date	Hour	Summary of Events and Information	Remarks and references to Appendices
In the field	13-XII-17		Hostile artillery more active. Special attention being paid to the valley running from VILLERS-PLOUICH to MARCOING. 2000 rds H.V. also direct rapid.	
"	14-XII-17		Hostile hostile aerial activity. 5000 rounds fired on E.A. & 2800 on direct rapid.	
"	15-XII-17		Coy was relieved by the 223 M.G. Coy. Relief was complete by 8.0 A.M.	
"	16-XII-17		Limbers thoroughly cleaned & Coy equipment prepared for a move	
"	17-XII-17		Coy marched to ETRICOURT & entrained at 10-0 A.M. When the coy detrained & marched to BEAUDRICOURT	
"	18-XII-17		The Coy left BEAUDRICOURT at 11.30 A.M. & marched to HUMBRICOURT	
"	19-XII-17		Inspection. Arms carried out & equipment was cleaned	
"	20-XII-17		Gun equipment cleaned. Mobilization Table checked	
"	21-XII-17		Route march. Lecture by C.O. 4 O.R. reinforcements joined	

Army Form C. 2118.

WAR DIARY
or
INTELLIGENCE SUMMARY.
(Erase heading not required.)

107th Coy M.G.C.

Place	Date	Hour	Summary of Events and Information	Remarks and references to Appendices
Field	22.XII.17	9B	Bgn. report to inspection route march	
"	23.XII.17	9/B	Church parade at 9.0 a.m. 11.0 a.m. POR reinforcements joined	
"	24.XII.17	9/B	Run. Coy Inspection at 9.0 — 11.0 a.m. Baths	
"	25.XII.17	9/B	Church Parade 9.15 a.m. under C.O.	
"	26.XII.17	9/B	Coy Inspection 11.0 a.m. Transport (8 limbers) moved to PUCH-VILLERS at 9.0 a.m. under T.O.	
"	27.XII.17	9W	Coy moved by train to CORBIE Area.	
"	28.XII.17	9W	Training under Section Officers	
"	29.XII.17	9W	" " "	
"	30.XII.17	9W	" " "	
"	31.XII.17	9W	" " "	

107 G M.G.C.   VIII 26

WAR DIARY
or
INTELLIGENCE SUMMARY.
(Erase heading not required.)

Army Form C. 2118.

Place	Date	Hour	Summary of Events and Information	Remarks and references to Appendices
	1st Jan 18	AM	Company barrage drill firing practice site selected for machine gun officers. 30 Rounds fired	
	2nd "	AM		
	3rd "	AM		
	4th "	AM		
	5th "	AM		
	6th "	AM		
	7th "	AM		30 OR entrained, joined [?]
	8th "	AM	Company moved by march route to YRELY. Wet day	
	9th "	AM	Strong day	
	10th "	AM	Company marched by march route to PARGNY. Slept in C. Billets. Cookers joined. Mules remounts used by 91st Trench Mtr Bty.	
	11th "	AM	Company moved by march route to AUBIGNY	
	12th "	AM	Company joined MG Coy 12th By Bgd. 2 new officers. St QUENTIN town guns visiting site Bde reinforcmt FONTAINE	

Army Form C. 2118.

WAR DIARY
or
INTELLIGENCE SUMMARY.
(Erase heading not required.)

107th O. M. G. C.

Place	Date	Hour	Summary of Events and Information	Remarks and references to Appendices
Field	13/1/18	am	Normal day, very quiet. 1 O.R. wounded, 6 O.R. other ranks returning by transport.	
	14/1/18	pm	Normal day. Enemy artillery more active. A.O.R. reinforcements joined.	
	15/1/18	am	Enemy artillery fairly active on night of Bde Sector.	
	16/1/18	pm	Enemy T.M's fairly active on night of Bde Sector M.G. & light T.M. activity at Stand to in the morning.	
	17/1/18	am	Quiet day a little artillery activity on night of Bde Sector.	
	18/1/18	pm	Our artillery more active during the day. Enemy M.G's active on which front during the night. Our aircraft very active. Enemy artillery shelled our right	
	19/1/18	pm	sector for about 30 minutes at 6.25 P.M.	
	20/1/18	pm	Aircraft active. Enemy artillery quiet. Unusual activity observed in the enemy's lines.	
	21/1/18	pm	Activity noticed yesterday continued today. But was dealt with by our artillery. At 4.30 P.M. enemy gave an unusual display of coloured lights no action followed. Enemy artillery inactive. About 11.0 P.M. enemy raiders on line and captured somewhere	
	22/1/18	am	in front By	

Army Form C. 2118.

WAR DIARY
or
INTELLIGENCE SUMMARY.
(Erase heading not required.)

107th Coy. M.G.C.

Place	Date	Hour	Summary of Events and Information	Remarks and references to Appendices
	22/1/18	A.M.	Enemy artillery very active shelled BRUGIES at 2.30 a.m. Enemy m.gs fired during the day in BRUGIES. At 9 p.m. our artillery put down a barrage in front of right battalion, in response to S.O.S. sent up by Coy on right	
	23/1/18	P.M.	Day + night normal, aircraft still active	
	24/1/18	A.M.	Day + night normal. The period very quiet no artillery activity	
	25/1/18	A.M.	Enemy machine guns rather more active, aircraft also active very quiet	
	26/1/18	P.M.	Thick mist all day. No activity at all	
	27/1/18	A.M.	Again misty in the morning, cleared in afternoon and both artilleries became active but only for a short period	
	28/1/18	A.M.	Clear day, great aerial activity on both sides artilleries active, enemy shelling our batteries and our repeating it. 2 enemy planes being brought down to our nearer lines. Bombing planes passed over at night	
	29/1/18	P.M.	Clear with early morning but got misty late. Little activity of any sort except aerial. Several squadrons of our enemy bombing planes passed over our lines about 8.30 p.m. Bombs were dropped in rear back areas.	

www.ingramcontent.com/pod-product-compliance
Lightning Source LLC
Chambersburg PA
CBHW081543160426
43191CB00011B/1829